access to politics

D0276454

THE PRIME MINISTER

and

CABINET GOVERNMENT

Neil McNaughton

Series Editor: David Simpson

Hodder & Stoughton

A MEMBER OF THE HODDER HEADLINE GROUP

ACKNOWLEDGEMENTS

The photos on pp 15, 50, 74, 83 and 87 are reproduced with permission of PA News.

Orders: please contact Bookpoint Ltd, 39 Milton Park, Abingdon, Oxon OX14 4TD. Telephone: (44) 01235 400414, Fax: (44) 01235 400454. Lines are open from 9.00–6.00, Monday to Saturday, with a 24 hour message answering service. Email address: orders@bookpoint.co.uk

A catalogue record for this title is available from The British Library

ISBN 0 340 747595

First published 1999
Impression number 10 9 8 7 6 5 4 3 2 1
Year   2004 2003 2002 2001 2000 1999

Cover photo from PA News

Typeset by Transet Limited, Coventry, England.
Printed in Great Britain for Hodder & Stoughton Educational, a division of Hodder Headline plc, 338 Euston Road, London NW1 3BH by Redwood Books, Trowbridge, Wilts.

CONTENTS

PREFACE

A/AS Level syllabuses in Government and Politics aim to develop knowledge and understanding of the political system of the UK. They cover its local, national and European Union dimensions, and include comparative studies of aspects of other political systems, in order to ensure an understanding of the distinctive nature of the British political system. The minimum requirements for comparative study are aspects of systems with a separation of powers, how other systems protect the rights of individuals and how other electoral systems work.

Access to Politics is a series of concise topic books which cover the syllabus requirements, providing students with the necessary resources to complete the course successfully.

General advice on approaching exam questions

To achieve high grades you need to demonstrate consistency. Clearly address all parts of a question, make good use of essay plans or notes, and plan your time to cover all the questions.

Make your answers stand out from the crowd by using contemporary material to illustrate them. You should read a quality newspaper and listen to or watch appropriate programmes on radio and television.

Skills Advice

You should comprehend, synthesise and interpret political information in a variety of forms:

- Analyse and evaluate political institutions, processes and behaviour, political arguments and explanations.
- Identify parallels, connections, similarities and differences between aspects of the political systems studied.
- Select and organise relevant material to construct arguments and explanations leading to reasoned conclusions.
- Communicate the arguments with relevance, clarity and coherence, using vocabulary appropriate to the study of Government and Politics.

David Simpson

1

INTRODUCTION

IN THIS CHAPTER the historical origins of both the Cabinet and the office of Prime Minister are traced back to the seventeenth century. The two institutions are closely related, so that the development of each must be seen in the light of the development of both. In 1867, Walter Bagehot summarised their importance at a key moment in the history of British politics – the passage of the Second Reform Act. Bagehot gives a clear insight into the true nature of Cabinet government which is still largely valid today.

Having contrasted the British Cabinet with its American counterpart, we place the Prime Minister in the context of modern politics, demonstrating its central position in the system. Finally there is a brief summary of the important reforms which are under way under Tony Blair's premiership.

Key Points:
- Origins of the Cabinet and office of Prime Minister
- Walter Bagehot's views, 1867
- The Prime Minister and Cabinet today.

ORIGINS OF THE CABINET

THE FIRST TRUE CABINETS

One of the original meanings of the word 'Cabinet' – a small room used for private consultations – tells us much about the origin of the British Cabinet. It was indeed a term used to describe the small group of advisers who gathered round the Monarch in the seventeenth century.

This body became semi-formalised in the joint reign of King William III and his wife Mary in the 1690s.

What do we mean by the term 'semi-formalised'? It is an important question because it can tell us the difference between the idea of a specific feature of the British system of government – which Cabinet government has become – and merely the tendency for powerful leaders to gather a group of close followers or disciples around them. The formal nature of William III's Cabinet lay in the fact that its members could collectively exercise some control over Parliament. Again though this development took place three centuries ago it helps us to understand why today's Cabinet is so important.

Before William and Mary took the throne after the Glorious Revolution of 1688 the Monarch did not need to exert any permanent control over Parliament. It was simply not significant enough a body. The Monarch reigned supreme and mostly used Parliament to add some legitimacy or authority to his or her decisions. True its support would be preferred and it increased the Monarch's power, but Parliament was not *needed* for much of the time. William III *did* need the support of Parliament in order to rule his newly acquired kingdom. The 1689 settlement, which established the new system of government, had shifted the balance of power – over both legislation and finance – towards Parliament and away from the Monarch.

So the group of mostly Whigs (the dominant parliamentary party of the time) whom William consulted and trusted, was invaluable to him. They could suggest which policies and actions would be acceptable to Parliament and which would not. Once a decision was reached they could help to ensure that Parliament would comply. In other words the Cabinet had developed a formal role in the workings of the government. It has never since lost this central position.

But we only used the term '*semi* formalised' above. We must be careful not to run away with the idea that today's Cabinet is basically the same as it was in 1690. It certainly did not have any rules of procedure, did not have a set membership and was not backed by any kind of formal party system. It was still a loose arrangement and remained so for some time.

UNDER HANOVERIAN KINGS

It is a curious but important fact of British history that George I, the first of the Kings from the German House of Hanover, was not especially delighted to find himself ruling England. His accession to the throne in 1714 was unexpected, having been caused by the failure of Queen Anne to produce a living adult heir despite 17 pregnancies. He spoke little English and was not especially interested in the politics of the country. He therefore often missed meetings of the Cabinet and even when he was there, could follow little of the discussions. As a result the Cabinet began its long evolution into the body we recognise today.

What had started to happen under George I was that the Cabinet began effectively to rule the country. This continued with relatively little interference under George II until George III began his long reign from 1760–1820. He considered himself a true English king rather than a German interloper and re-established some control. He spoke English and attended meetings regularly. More importantly he led the discussions and largely determined their outcome. In some ways indeed George III played the modern role that we know as prime minister until his famed intermittent insanity became permanent after 1811. There were by this time senior ministers already known as prime minister, but the modern functions of the office which we know today and which are described in detail in the rest of this book were exercised then by the Monarch. He or she appointed or dismissed the ministers, set the agenda for discussion and could still make some decisions without consulting the Cabinet, and often did. This was the situation until 1832.

PARLIAMENTARY SUPREMACY

In 1832 the Great Reform Act established a number of key developments in the British political system. The changes had a major impact upon the position of the Cabinet. The main features of reform were as follows:

- A regularised system of voting and constituency representation was established for the House of Commons.
- Because the Commons was to be properly and more democratically elected it became a more influential body than the unelected House of Lords. Though in theory the two Houses had equal powers to make and amend laws, after 1832 the Commons was the stronger partner.
- The more organised voting system quickly led to the establishment of formal, unified parties which were increasingly able to dominate debates in the House of Commons.

These changes deeply affected the role and composition of the Cabinet. We can also condense these down to three developments:

- Cabinet ministers were increasingly drawn from the House of Commons rather than the Lords, reflecting the growing authority of the elected chamber.
- The authority and influence of the Monarch (for most of this period Queen Victoria) declined as the importance of Parliament, especially the Commons, grew.
- There was an increasing tendency for one of the parties to be in a dominant position (though not holding an absolute majority of MPs as has been the case since 1945) in the Commons. This meant that such parties would also control Cabinet membership. As a result the Monarch lost control over Cabinet composition.

The Monarch had gradually ceased to attend Cabinet meetings. As we shall see below, this coincided with the growing importance of the office of Prime Minister.

The nature of Cabinet government and the position of Prime Minister after 1867 can now be considered. From this time it becomes increasingly difficult to separate discussion of the two institutions. In other words they became irrevocably intertwined.

ORIGINS OF THE OFFICE OF PRIME MINISTER

ROBERT WALPOLE

Nearly every school pupil who paid any attention to history lessons will be able to name Robert Walpole as Britain's first ever Prime Minister. In 1721 he became First Lord of the Treasury. Yet the year in which he became prime minister in the true sense of the term was 1729. The uncertainty surrounding the founding date of the office results from the fact that there was never an Act of Parliament passed nor any other document published which created the post. Indeed the term had been used before 1729 and it was only inconsistently applied to Walpole after 1729. So why Walpole, and why 1729?

The answer to these questions tells us much about the nature of the office even today. A number of developments coincided to create the position of prime minister:

- The first two Hanoverian Kings had relatively little interest in politics and so delegated much of their power to a minister – naturally the First or Prime Minister.
- There was at that time a reasonably unified party of MPs and peers, the Whigs, who could be relied upon to support an individual minister who best represented their philosophy and political goals. Walpole was that man in 1729.
- In 1729, Walpole's great rival, Lord Townshend, resigned, having lost the confidence of the King. This meant that Walpole could take over his responsibilities and combine the positions of First Lord of the Treasury (in charge of financial affairs) and First Minister (in charge of foreign and domestic policy). He had in other words created an office with wide powers over public policy. It is an historical curiosity incidentally that the official title of the Prime Minister is still First Lord of the Treasury.

All this is not merely historical background. The story illustrates nicely the position of prime minister to this day. In practice this means that he or she combines five essential characteristics just as Walpole did, though on a greater scale. The Prime Minister:

1 exercises a number of powers delegated to him or her by the Monarch. These are known as prerogative powers.
2 largely determines the composition of the Cabinet.
3 is able to lead and maintain a unified Cabinet which can present a coherent programme and a confident face to Parliament.

4 must be able to demonstrate that he or she commands the support of a majority in Parliament, (nowadays specifically the House of Commons).

5 has sufficient political authority and ability to become chief policy-maker across the whole range of government business.

These are truths which apply to Tony Blair as much as they did to Walpole. The system may be more complex today, the powers of the Monarchy may have all but disappeared and the party system may be considerably more formal, but the fundamentals of the office are basically the same.

ROBERT PEEL

Most political historians are agreed that the first Prime Minister in the truly modern sense of the word was Robert Peel, who held office as leader of the Conservatives in 1834–5, and again in 1841–6. What was it about Peel which had changed the office?

The first answer lies in the role of the Cabinet. As we have seen above, after the 1832 Great Reform Act the Cabinet had gained considerably in political importance and influence. It was natural therefore that the leader of the Cabinet, the Prime Minister, should also gain authority. Peel, at least in his second term of office, led a unified Conservative Party (he is often considered to be the founder of the modern Conservative Party). This gave him great personal control over Parliament, which his contemporary, Benjamin Disraell, said he could 'play like an old fiddle.'

Secondly he, above all his predecessors, enjoyed widespread personal popularity. Most people still did not have the right to vote in the 1840s, but there is little doubt that he would have topped any poll at the time had there been full elections. His repeal of the Corn Laws, which brought down food prices and improved the condition of the working classes, was the principal basis of his popularity.

Thirdly he enjoyed the confidence of the Queen, the young Victoria. She was still learning the business of politics and so had to rely heavily upon him.

So Peel was a genuine party leader controlling a genuine political party; he could claim to be the voice of the people, at least of the majority and he could usually ensure that his, his Cabinet's and his party's policies would be approved by Parliament. Modern prime ministers must enjoy very similar advantages if they are to succeed.

WALTER BAGEHOT'S VIEWS, 1867

Walter Bagehot, journalist and editor of *The Economist* magazine, wrote in 1867 a work entitled *The English Constitution*. In it he described the British political system as he understood it to work at that time. Since Britain has no written Constitution of the kind which France or the USA has it is necessary to use writings like Bagehot's to help us understand the system. Though written over a century ago Bagehot's work remains useful, especially in explaining the nature and role of two of the country's central institutions – prime minister and Cabinet. In particular he concentrates upon the key feature which can explain their position, that is the relationship between government and Parliament.

GOVERNMENT AND PARLIAMENT

We can define government as the part of the system which makes policies, decides how they are to be implemented, and coordinates the achievement of those policies. This involves mainly the Cabinet, its attached bodies, and the great departments of state which are led by the ministers who make up that Cabinet.

Parliament on the other hand is a body whose main role is to represent the people in the granting of approval for those policies developed in government and, occasionally, to withhold approval, thus asking government to think again or even abandon its plans.

Walter Bagehot recognised that these roles could and would inevitably cause conflict. There was a danger indeed that conflict could become deadlock and the whole system would cease to function. There was no written Constitution to show a way through such problems, to resolve the conflicts. It was, he revealed, the role of the Cabinet with a prime minister at its head to avoid such logjams. It provides a bridge between government and Parliament ensuring that such conflict is rare, and is certainly controlled. He famously called this part of the system the 'efficient secret', in other words the mechanism which makes it really work.

As far as the office of prime minister was concerned Bagehot described him or her as *'primus inter pares'* within the Cabinet. This Latin term means 'first among equals'. What he meant was that the Prime Minister was at the same time head of the Cabinet and a simple member like all the others, with the same amount of influence. He or she could try to direct the Cabinet, but could also be over-ruled by them.

Walter Bagehot was right to be imprecise about the Prime Minister's relationship to his or her own Cabinet. It has been the subject of fervent academic discussion ever since. This discussion will be summarised in this book in Chapters 5 and 6. However, it is worth noting here that after Harold Macmillan's premiership, which ran from 1957–63, the balance of opinion began to shift towards the idea that the Prime Minister has come to dominate Cabinet government to an ever-increasing extent.

THE EFFICIENT SECRET

Of course what Bagehot really meant was that the Cabinet is able to control what Parliament does for most of the time. By commanding the agenda, business and, to some extent, voting in the House it can reduce to a minimum the possibility that its wishes will be thwarted. It is also true that this control is not exercised against the will of Parliament. On the whole the majority party in Parliament willingly allows the Cabinet, which is also its own parliamentary leadership, to dominate it. We may call this decisive government or 'elective dictatorship' as Lord Hailsham did in 1976, but Bagehot's description as the 'efficient secret' is perhaps best.

If we take the words directly from Bagehot's The *English Constitution* we can find a vivid description of Cabinet's importance along these lines:

A cabinet is a combining committee – a hyphen which joins, a buckle which fastens, the legislative part of the state [Parliament] to the executive part of the state [Government].

Although the party system is even more rigid today than it was in Bagehot's day and though the Prime Minister is a more dominant figure, this analogy remains accurate. Much of this book will explore the nature of the control of prime minister and Cabinet over Parliament, but it is worth pausing here to make a comparison with the situation which pertains in the USA.

CONTRAST WITH THE USA

The American Constitution does not have such an efficient secret. Instead the powers of the legislature (Congress) and the government (the President and the appointed administration) are very evenly balanced. Conflict between them is common, and gridlock is a constant feature of the system. There *is* such a thing as the Cabinet in the USA, but it does not provide a link with Congress. American Cabinet members are not allowed to be members of Congress and certainly do not exercise any discipline or direction over its elected members. Even the President, who has been directly elected by the people, cannot claim any great authority over Congress. In other words the system is not as efficient as Britain's. This does not necessarily mean of course that the Americans would wish to change it. Most prefer it the way it is.

THE PRIME MINISTER AND CABINET TODAY

All the developments described above are helpful to our understanding of the modern Prime Minister and Cabinet. But if we are to establish when the institutions truly came into existence in the form in which we see them today, the year 1916 is perhaps our best starting point.

LLOYD GEORGE AND MAURICE HANKEY

When David Lloyd George succeeded Herbert Asquith as Liberal prime minister in the middle of the First World War, he had already decided that both the way the Cabinet worked and the Prime Minister's relationship to it, had to change. This was not just because the war effort needed better administration; Lloyd George had his eye also on post-war Britain and the radical reforms he hoped to achieve. Though Bagehot had described the Cabinet system as 'efficient' nearly 50 years before, it was not efficient enough for Lloyd George's liking.

He employed a civil servant and former army officer, Maurice Hankey, to reform the Cabinet system. The principal developments which Hankey made under Lloyd George's careful direction were:

- A formal record or minutes of Cabinet meetings was to be kept and circulated to those in government who needed to know.
- It followed from the above that there was to be a clear record also of all decisions made in Cabinet.
- A system of sub-committees or simply Cabinet committees was established. These would consider specialised areas of policy and recommend action to the full Cabinet. The committees contained small groups of ministers from both inside and outside the Cabinet. The Prime Minister would chair the most important ones.
- The formal office of Cabinet secretary was set up (Hankey was its first incumbent). He or she would be the government's most senior civil servant and would have the formal task of organising the Cabinet's business and the informal one of helping to maintain Cabinet unity.
- The Cabinet Secretary would head a Cabinet secretariat also staffed by civil servants. Their most important role was to ensure that the government as a whole – that is all ministers and senior civil servants – should know and understand all Cabinet decisions.

This is largely how the British Cabinet is organised to this day. There are more committees and the Cabinet Secretary and his office's roles have expanded, but this is the *system* we have now.

In addition Lloyd George wished to underpin his own power as prime minister. To help him he created a secretariat of close advisers who served him alone. This was known at the time as the 'Garden Suburb' because its offices were set up in the gardens of 10 Downing Street. Though this institution did not survive Lloyd George, it was the forerunner of the wide variety of sources of prime-ministerial advice which now proliferate at the centre of government.

PERIOD	PRIME MINISTER	CABINET
\multicolumn{3}{c}{**Table 1:** *Historical development of Prime Minister and Cabinet*}		
Pre 1689	No such office	A very loose group of advisers to the Monarch
1689–1714	Effectively the Monarch was prime minister	Cabinet develops political unity and begins to share power with the Monarch
1714–1832	Prime-ministerial office evolves. Prime minister becomes cabinet leader, sharing power with the Monarch	
1832–67	Prime minister gains power at the expense of the Monarch	Political power shifts away from the Monarch and is taken over by prime minister and cabinet. Cabinet exerts increasing control over House of Commons majority
1867–1916	Prime minister increasingly able to exert control over Parliament	
1916–57	Prime minister leads a unified cabinet and exerts discipline over members	Modern Cabinet system develops
1957–present	So-called 'era of prime-ministerial government'	

THE 'DIGNIFIED' AND THE 'EFFICIENT'

The institutions of the modern Cabinet system and office of prime minister were largely created together in 1916. Since then they have occupied the centre ground of the British political scene. We will examine the reasons why this is so in some detail below, but at this stage we can allow Bagehot again to set the scene.

Walter Bagehot distinguished between what he called the 'dignified' parts of the political system and the 'efficient' elements. What he meant by 'dignified' was that there were some institutions which *appeared* to be very grand and important, but they were in fact largely for show; they were merely ceremonial. The most obvious example is the Monarchy. Today as much as in Bagehot's day the Queen presides over many great political occasions – the state opening of Parliament in autumn; the Queen's Speech at that opening, when she details the government's programme of action for the next 12 months, the formal installation of the Prime Minister after a general election; presiding at official visits by foreign heads of state; and many other similar occasions. They have no real political significance, but they remain impressive demonstrations of the splendour of the State.

If he were writing today Bagehot would add to the list of dignified parts much of the work of the House of Commons. The great debates on legislation, Prime Minister's Question Time, ministerial announcements and the like do appear as dazzling as other state occasions, but they are largely a ritual. The *real* work of governing has already been largely completed. Decisions are made elsewhere and most parliamentary occasions are simply the public confirmation of those decisions. They are, in short, *symbols* of the democratic process. But they *are* nevertheless still very necessary. The people need both the reassurance that MPs remain the guardians of our rights and interests and to be impressed by the grandeur of those whom we have entrusted with the levers of government.

But where does the efficient secret lie today? What is the real centre of the governing process?

CENTRAL PLACE OF PRIME MINISTER AND CABINET SYSTEM

Very few students of politics would have a problem in placing the Prime Minister in such a central position. Since Lloyd George all prime ministers for most of the time have placed themselves at the core of the political system. It is true that there were times when Stanley Baldwin in the 1920s, Clement Attlee in the 1940s, and Winston Churchill in extreme old age and ill-health did take something of a back seat, but for most of the time the Prime Minister remains at the hub of government.

The position of the Cabinet is not so clear. As we shall see below, there is much evidence to suggest that the Cabinet itself, in the form of 20 or so of the most senior ministers who meet once a week for two or three hours in secret session, may have lost its central role. There are authoritative views which suggest that the formal Cabinet is now one of the dignified parts of the political process. However, if we think of Cabinet as the centre of a whole *system* of decision-making and advisory bodies it is still widely held that this is indeed part of the efficient secret. It is therefore important to distinguish between the *Cabinet* as such and the *Cabinet system*, which is a more accurate term today.

THE BLAIR REFORMS

The changes which have been made under Blair's premiership in 1997–8 are described in some detail below. They appear to constitute a major development in the position of the Prime Minister and in particular his or her relationship with a newly empowered Cabinet Office.

There is now a powerful group of ministers, advisers and officials headed by the Prime Minister who are able to consider, refine, present and enforce new policies. Prime ministers have always fought shy of using civil servants for their own purposes; it has been felt in the past that this would jeopardise the neutrality of the civil service. This has changed. There is now a significant group of officials whose specific role is to serve the Prime Minister in his role as chief policy maker.

PRIME MINISTER AND CABINET IN THE
DECISION-MAKING PROCESS

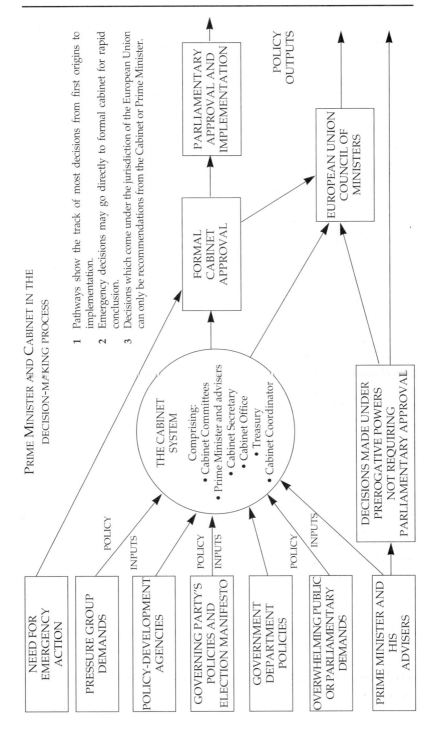

1 Pathways show the track of most decisions from first origins to implementation.
2 Emergency decisions may go directly to formal cabinet for rapid conclusion.
3 Decisions which come under the jurisdiction of the European Union can only be recommendations from the Cabinet or Prime Minister.

POLICY OUTPUTS

PARLIAMENTARY APPROVAL AND IMPLEMENTATION

FORMAL CABINET APPROVAL

EUROPEAN UNION COUNCIL OF MINISTERS

DECISIONS MADE UNDER PREROGATIVE POWERS NOT REQUIRING PARLIAMENTARY APPROVAL

THE CABINET SYSTEM

Comprising;
• Cabinet Committees
• Prime Minister and advisers
• Cabinet Secretary
• Cabinet Office
• Treasury
• Cabinet Coordinator

POLICY

INPUTS

POLICY

INPUTS

POLICY

INPUTS

NEED FOR EMERGENCY ACTION

PRESSURE GROUP DEMANDS

POLICY-DEVELOPMENT AGENCIES

GOVERNING PARTY'S POLICIES AND ELECTION MANIFESTO

GOVERNMENT DEPARTMENT POLICIES

OVERWHELMING PUBLIC OR PARLIAMENTARY DEMANDS

PRIME MINISTER AND HIS ADVISERS

Tony Blair has also widened the opportunity for the Prime Minister to bring outsiders into his or her own inner circle of government. There is therefore a four-cornered establishment at his disposal. This consists of his personal advisers, a group of senior civil servants in the Cabinet Office including the Cabinet Secretary, two senior Cabinet colleagues – the Cabinet Office Minister and Leader of the House of Commons – and a range of policy units which report directly to the Prime Minister. In the following chapter we will put these changes into context.

The position of the Prime Minister, Cabinet and its wider system are illustrated on page 11.

SUMMARY

The key points which need to be emphasised are as follows:

- The institutions of prime minister and Cabinet have been steadily evolving over three centuries. Their functions and powers are not covered by any parliamentary statute or constitutional document.
- Since Bagehot's day, Cabinet has provided the key link between government and Parliament.
- There is no doubt that the Prime Minister and Cabinet government stand at the centre of the political process, although doubts have been cast about the importance of the formal Cabinet itself.
- Since 1916 there has been a wider Cabinet system in operation.
- The relationship between the Prime Minister and the rest of the government remains ambiguous.
- The reforms being pushed through by Blair appear to represent a crucial change in the nature of government at the centre.

Revision Hints

Notes should be taken on the following key areas:

- The manner in which the two institutions have evolved was the result of various historical developments. These key developments should be noted.
- An intimate knowledge of Bagehot is not required, but a basic knowledge of his principal conclusions is useful introductory material. This especially applies to the relationship between government and Parliament, and the difference between the efficient and dignified parts of the system.
- You should have a knowledge of the Cabinet system which was first created by Hankey in 1916, as it still largely applies today.

Exam Hints

At this stage you will not have sufficient information to be able to answer detailed questions on the Prime Minister and Cabinet. However, the way in which these institutions have evolved can be employed as a useful example of how the British Constitution itself has simply evolved rather than been created. Indeed, Bagehot's *The English Constitution* is often quoted as an example of a book of authority which is an important source of Britain's unwritten Constitution.

The ambiguous position of both the Prime Minister and the Cabinet in the British system of government may certainly be used in questions inviting you to discuss the need or otherwise for a written Constitution to clarify the position.

2

HOW THE CABINET WORKS

Introduction

HERE WE EXAMINE the real nature of the modern Cabinet, beginning with an explanation of how its membership is determined. The functions and responsibilities of the Cabinet are then described. The organisation of the broader Cabinet *system* is discussed and explained. This section includes an exposition of the nature and work of Cabinet committees, together with a variety of other support bodies of both a management and political nature.

Some of these bodies are part of the extensive innovations to the Cabinet system which are being introduced under Tony Blair's supervision. Finally the doctrine of *collective cabinet responsibility* is defined and its importance emphasised. This is the principle which does most to ensure that Cabinet government works effectively.

Key Points:
- Function and role of the Cabinet
- Cabinet committees and system
- Collective Cabinet responsibility.

WHAT IS THE CABINET?

There are three sub-questions here. Firstly who are they? Secondly why are some chosen and not others? Finally what is the position of the Cabinet in the British Constitution?

TONY BLAIR'S CABINET AT DOWNING STREET

WHO IS IN THE CABINET?

Every government contains over 100 ministers who have a specific role, all of them selected either from the House of Commons or the House of Lords. It should be stressed here that ministers *retain* their positions in either House of Parliament even though they become ministers. All these ministers are appointed by the Prime Minister (though parliamentary private secretaries, PPSs, who are unpaid assistants to ministers are selected from either House by those ministers rather than the Prime Minister).

Among those ministers there are between 20–25 senior members who form the Cabinet, the inner circle of the government. Here there is no exception to the rule that it is the Prime Minister alone who decides which ministers should be in the Cabinet. There are two types of Cabinet minister. Firstly there are those who head a government department. Secondly there are ministers who do not have the burden of a department, but handle some aspects of the government's *political* business.

We can make a further distinction between those who hold posts which *always* carry Cabinet status such as chancellor of the exchequer and foreign secretary, and those who might or might not be included, such as minister for transport.

The table below shows the Labour Party Cabinet as selected by Tony Blair in January 1999. It also indicates from which House of Parliament they come and whether they are heads of department or political managers.

Table 2: *The Cabinet, 1.1.99*

MINISTER	POSITION	FROM WHICH HOUSE OF PARLIAMENT?	DEPARTMENT HEAD OR MANAGER?	IS THIS POST ALWAYS IN CABINET?
Tony Blair	Prime Minister	Commons	Manager	Yes
John Prescott	Environment and Transport	Commons	Both*	Yes
Gordon Brown	Chancellor the the Exchequer	Commons	Both	Yes
Robin Cook	Foreign Secretary	Commons	Department	Yes
Margaret Becket	Leader of the Commons	Commons	Manager	Yes
George Robertson	Defence	Commons	Department	Yes
Stephen Byers	Trade and Industry	Commons	Department	Yes
Lord Irvine	Lord Chancellor	Lords	Department	Yes
Baroness Jay	Leader of the Lords	Lords	Manager	Yes
Jack Cunningham	Cabinet Office	Commons	Manager	No
Chris Smith	National Heritage	Commons	Department	No
Ann Taylor	Chief Whip	Commons	Manager	No**
Mo Mowlem	Northern Ireland Secretary	Commons	Department	Yes
Donald Dewar	Scottish Secretary	Commons	Department	Yes
Alun Michael	Welsh Secretary	Commons	Department	Yes
Nick Brown	Agriculture and Food	Commons	Department	No
David Blunkett	Education and Employment	Commons	Department	Yes
Alastair Darling	Social Security	Commons	Department	Yes
Alan Milburn	Chief Treasury Secretary	Commons	Both□	Yes
Jack Straw	Home Secretary	Commons	Department	Yes
Clare Short	Overseas Development	Commons	Department	No
Frank Dobson	Health	Commons	Department	Yes

Notes: * John Prescott was deputy prime minister and so was also a manager.
** Even when the Chief Whip is NOT strictly a cabinet member he or she always attends meetings. In 1999 however, she was a full member.
□ Though an assistant to the Chancellor of the Exchequer he oversees department spending and so is also a manager.

It should also be noted that non-Cabinet ministers may be invited to take part in discussions where they may have a particularly valuable contribution, but they will not be permitted to take a part in the final decision and will only attend for that part of the business which concerns them. After 1998 for example, the Chief Whip in the House of Lords and the Transport Secretary were both required to attend all meetings without being formal members. The Cabinet Secretary, who is a neutral civil servant and not a politician at all, also attends every meeting to record the decisions made and to ensure that procedures are followed. He or she also does not take part in decision-making. After the meeting the Cabinet Secretary ensures that the necessary people – in the government and among the civil servants – know what Cabinet has decided.

WHY ARE SOME CHOSEN?

Since Cabinet ministers have a dual role – they are Cabinet members but also have a role as a department head or a government manager – the Prime Minister may appoint them for one of two basic reasons:

1 He or she may primarily want them in the Cabinet in the inner circle, in which case a job of senior enough status to warrant a Cabinet post must be found for them. This was certainly the case with Peter Mandelson's short-lived elevation to Cabinet membership in July 1998 (he resigned in December 1998).

2 He or she may want an individual to fill a particular role – for example chancellor of the exchequer – in which case that person will automatically be in the Cabinet because the holder of that post always has that high status. Gordon Brown was such an individual when Blair came to power in 1997.

But it is not as simple as this. The Prime Minister is also building a **team** when Cabinet is appointed. This team will run the government. The eyes of Parliament, the media and the public will be on that group. They will make key decisions so that the fortunes of the government largely depend upon their performance. There may be a number of considerations on the Prime Minister's mind when selecting individuals for the team. These are identified below along with some examples:

• He or she may be an old trusted ally of the Prime Minister. This was the case when Blair appointed Lord Irvine as Lord Chancellor in 1997.

• The appointee may be a potential troublemaker who could stir up opposition to the government from its own back-benchers in the Commons. By being placed in the Cabinet he or she will effectively be gagged (this is related to the doctrine of collective Cabinet responsibility which is described below in Chapter 3). This was one reason why John Major's 1992–7 Cabinet contained Michael Portillo.

• An individual may have the support of a particular faction within the party. In order to satisfy that faction, its leading member may be invited into the

Cabinet. This played a part in John Prescott's appointment as Deputy Prime Minister in 1997. He represented 'old' or traditional Labour in contrast to the 'New' Labour movement of Blair.

• In some cases there is someone who is so talented as a politician and minister that the Prime Minister wants that person in a senior position because he or she will be an asset to the Government. Such Cabinet ministers as Mo Mowlem (Labour in the 1990s) or William Whitelaw (Conservative in the 1970s and 80s) probably fall into this category.

Before we summarise the art of Cabinet building it should be pointed out that where a party has been in opposition and then wins an election the Prime Minister is not entirely free to choose his or her own Cabinet. The Opposition Party always has a shadow Cabinet – a kind of government-in-waiting. In the case of the Labour Party this body is elected by all the MPs, whereas the Conservative shadow team is selected by the party leader. In either eventuality a newly elected prime minister must start with *most* of the Cabinet team which was chosen in opposition. In other words he or she is not entirely free to choose all the members. Once in power for some time however, Prime Ministers can feel free enough to make their own choice. This was certainly the case for Margaret Thatcher in 1981–2 (having been originally elected in 1979) and for Blair in 1998 (after his 1997 election).

Essentially therefore there are two basic kinds of Cabinet:

• A balanced Cabinet containing members with a variety of political philosophies to keep all sections of the ruling party happy. This was the case with James Callaghan (1976–9), Thatcher (1979–82) and Major (1990–7).
• A prime minister's Cabinet full of close supporters of their leader who represent a single dominant philosophy within the party. This was true of Thatcher's Cabinets from 1982–90 and Blair's Cabinet after 1998.

Not unexpectedly the second type of Cabinet tends to be more stable than the former!

CABINET'S POSITION IN THE BRITISH CONSTITUTION

This is a more difficult question to answer than it seems at first sight. We shall see below that it is certainly possible to identify what Cabinet *does*, but establishing its *status* is problematic. Before attempting to do this we need to distinguish between the **government** and the **cabinet**. Government is a broad term comprising all those individuals and bodies which are *directly* involved in policy formulation and decision-making. The Cabinet is specifically 20 or so senior ministers who have been appointed by the Prime Minister. They are in a sense the 'board of directors' of the government. This can be summarised as follows:

Government   The Prime Minister.

The individuals and bodies who advise the Prime Minister.

All ministers whether in the Cabinet or not.

The senior civil servants in all government departments (though their role is anonymous).

All other bodies which provide direct political support for government.

Cabinet   The 20–25 ministers who are members of the House of Commons or the House of Lords and who are selected by the Prime Minister. They are at the centre of government.

If we simplify the decision-making process in Britain to its most basic description, there is a solution to our puzzle. With very few exceptions most important decisions in British politics are made either by the Prime Minister under the royal prerogative which delegated the Monarch's powers to him or her, or by the government in its widest sense or by the Cabinet itself. The Cabinet's responsibility depends upon who has made the decision. Thus we can establish three constitutional roles:

1   It can act as a control mechanism over prime-ministerial power.
2   It is a clearing house which ratifies decisions made within the rest of government. Without Cabinet approval a decision has no authority and will not be accepted.
3   Under some circumstances the Cabinet itself makes decisions, such as in a crisis or where government experiences deadlock.

But these constitutional duties are not the full story. Cabinet has other political tasks. These together with a more detailed examination of its constitutional roles are described in the next section.

FUNCTIONS OF THE CABINET

It is an immensely difficult task to define precisely what the Cabinet does or, more specifically, what it is meant to do. This is partly because Britain has no written Constitution to define its role and partly because the Cabinet is so subject to the way in which a prime minister wishes to govern. Peter Hennessy has summed this problem up:

Living as we do under a system of government without precise rules for the conduct of affairs that are formally agreed and made public – a system largely free of both regulations and referees – it is very difficult, at any given moment, to know what norms of behaviour and procedure are thought to be proper and necessary for the exercise of genuine Cabinet government.
Source: Peter Hennessy, *The Hidden Wiring*, Gollancz, 1995

But despite Hennessy's warning we can, by examining the many accounts which have been written about Cabinet government, establish an accurate catalogue of functions.

A shorthand summary of the functions described above is as follows:

- Developing the government agenda and programme
- Crisis management
- Media and public opinion management
- Settling ministerial disputes
- Legitimising important government decisions
- Acting as a balance to prime-ministerial power
- Overseeing relations with the European Union.

DEVELOPING THE GOVERNMENT'S AGENDA

No government can do everything it wishes to do and to honour all its election manifesto promises straight away. It has limited resources and must therefore make hard decisions about what it can do within those constraints. The principal limitations are:

- **Money**: Most policy initiatives require large amounts of public expenditure. This is self-evidently restricted and Cabinet is the ultimate arbiter of how this should be distributed among competing demands. It should be pointed out here that Cabinet is in fact constrained by two factors. Firstly there is the primacy of the Treasury which has enormous influence over this distribution of funds. Secondly in 1998 a new system was introduced whereby the government's main spending plans were set for three years in advance. This clearly reduces the Cabinet's role to simply making smaller annual adjustments.
- **Policy development and drafting time**: Most of the government's policies require detailed analysis, planning and usually the careful drafting of legislation. The civil servants and other bodies which undertake this work would quickly become overloaded if too much legislation were proposed at the same time.
- **Parliamentary time**: Wherever an actual Act of Parliament is required to implement policy – and this is usually the case – the government's business managers must estimate how long the legislation will take and how much parliamentary time is available. Only a small number of major bills can be introduced in any one year (it should be noted here that a bill must be passed by Parliament within a year to become a valid statute).

So every summer the Cabinet meets to decide what pieces of legislation will be in the Queen's Speech. This takes place at the state opening of Parliament in late autumn. The significance of this occasion is that it begins a parliamentary session. Any bills which have not completed all the required parliamentary procedures by the *end* of a session are lost. The new session begins after the state opening and the new bills can then be introduced. The Queen's Speech is written effectively by the Cabinet following their discussions. It announces which pieces of legislation – in other words which policies – have reached the front of the queue. Naturally ministers want their *own* policies to be enacted as soon as possible so these agenda discussions are particularly crucial and may become heated.

Each week, too, Cabinet discusses what will happen for the next seven days: what debates are due in both Houses, which ministers will speak, what announcements are due to be made, by whom and how will they be released.

In some cases of course Cabinet may have to abandon a policy altogether. This may be officially announced, but more likely the plans will simply be postponed until they eventually disappear off the agenda altogether.

DEALING WITH EMERGENCIES AND CRISES

This role is self-evident. Whereas agenda-planning relates to *known* commitments there may also be many unforeseen events which are so important and require such drastic action that only the Cabinet can make the necessary decision.

Nevertheless Cabinet does share this role with the Prime Minister and his or her advisers. Any military action is technically in the hands of the Prime Minister who exercises the prerogative power of commander-in-chief of the armed forces on behalf of the Monarch. Thus for example it was Thatcher and a small group of close associates who conducted the Falklands War in 1982. On the other hand the commitment of peace-keeping troops to Bosnia in the 1990s was largely a collective Cabinet decision, rather than John Major's alone.

Peacetime examples of urgent Cabinet action in unforeseen circumstances include:

- The crisis over BSE (Mad Cow Disease) and its human equivalent disease, CJD, in the 1990s.
- The IRA bombing campaign in Britain in the early 1980s.
- The collapse in the value of the pound sterling on the foreign exchange markets in 1992.

In each case a decisive response from the government was required. Only the Cabinet as a body has the necessary collective authority to be able to act.

A COMMON GOVERNMENT MESSAGE FOR THE MEDIA AND PARLIAMENT

With the growth in media attention on politics since the 1960s and especially in the 1990s there is immense pressure upon any government to present a positive and united image to the country. Before this development it was largely

Parliament which was concerned with examining the performance of government. This was relatively easy. Maintaining discipline and coherence in the sheltered and relatively sedate setting of Westminster was less of a problem than dealing with the modern intrusive and high-pressure tactics of broadcasters and journalists.

So the regular Cabinet meetings include sessions on how politics will be presented and try to ensure that the Cabinet speaks with a common voice. Problems need to be anticipated, awkward questions predicted and political tactics coordinated. Clearly this has been an easier task in a united Cabinet such as Blair's, or Thatcher's after 1982, than it was for Major's split Cabinet of 1992–7.

Under Blair this function has been further streamlined with a weekly planning meeting of the Prime Minister with his close advisers and a daily strategy meeting led by his lieutenant, the Minister for the Cabinet Office. These meetings are designed to ensure that presentation is controlled *on a daily basis*. The full Cabinet will only be required to discuss longer-term issues of policy presentation.

SETTLING DISPUTES BETWEEN MINISTERS

On the whole a prime minister would prefer that any problems between senior ministers should not reach Cabinet level. He or she, or the Cabinet Secretary, or the Cabinet Co-ordinator (a post which has largely developed in the 1990s) will work hard to avoid the need for such a decision.

However, if they fail, the Cabinet can act as a final high court in which the conflict is resolved. The most important kind of dispute occurs between various departments and the Treasury. It can happen that a minister's plans are thwarted by the Treasury's refusal to release the necessary funds. Here it is the role of the First Secretary to the Treasury (effectively the Chancellor of the Exchequer's Assistant) to resolve the problem, but if that fails Cabinet will decide. The Treasury usually wins. This is partly because its head, the Chancellor, is always a very senior minister who enjoys the confidence of the Prime Minister and partly because it is difficult for a departmental minister to find allies in such a situation. Other departments know that if a rival does win a financial battle with the Treasury the money may well come out of their own budget!

RECOMMENDATIONS OF COMMITTEES AND DEPARTMENTS

Although the approval of recommendations by committees and government departments is possibly the key role played by the Cabinet, it may well take the least time. It is not expected that the Cabinet should engage in lengthy detailed discussion of policy. If it did, it would have to be in virtually continuous session!

Instead Cabinet's role in this sense is to give the official stamp of political authority upon decisions. In this sense Cabinet is very much a 'dignified' part of the Constitution, as Bagehot would have put it. Occasionally of course, Cabinet may reject a proposal, but this would be very rare especially in a united government. More likely but also unusually, there might be a reference back to a committee, a request for further changes or for a major rethink. Normally however, this is a ritual which does not greatly exercise the attention of ministers. Indeed if there is likely to be a Cabinet dispute the Prime Minister or one of his or her business managers will normally intercept the proposal and send it back. This was certainly the case with reform of the welfare system, a potential minefield for Cabinet in 1998.

Since 1979 when Cabinet began to lose some of its status under Margaret Thatcher – a prime minister who willingly admitted that she mistrusted Cabinet government – the relationship between full Cabinet and its committees has changed. It is now accepted that many decisions will be made by committees and will be treated *as though* they were decisions of full Cabinet. This is described more fully in the section on Cabinet committees below. However, any key elements of government policy which have been considered by a committee *must* be ratified by full Cabinet.

DECISIONS MADE BY THE PRIME MINISTER

It is not strictly necessary for the Prime Minister to consult Cabinet over decisions which he or she has the authority to make. Normally concerning national security, warfare and negotiations with foreign powers, these areas fall within the royal prerogative not Cabinet government. However, it would be a rash prime minister who never consulted senior colleagues over key decisions.

Margaret Thatcher, if some of her former ministers are to be believed, certainly did make decisions over the heads of her Cabinet and for the most part was powerful enough to survive their displeasure. But in the end she fell from power because the same Cabinet members refused to support her in a leadership challenge in November 1990. Her failure to consult them meaningfully, rebounded on her in the end. Similarly another Conservative prime minister, Edward Heath, chose to put economic policy into reverse in 1971–2 and did so with the cooperation of a few close colleagues, but without full discussion with either the Cabinet or his back-bench MPs. Though he was not ousted in the way that Thatcher was, he did lose much credibility within his party.

Very occasionally the Cabinet may over-rule a prime minister. Even the dominant Thatcher was forced by a determined Cabinet to bring Britain into the European Exchange Rate Mechanism (the ill-fated ERM which fixed the value of the pound sterling against European currencies) in 1990. John Major's fragile hold over a Cabinet which was hopelessly split over Europe and economic policy led to his inability to conduct any negotiations with his European counterparts without their approval.

But the likelihood of a defiant Cabinet should not be overstated. It is normally the case that the Prime Minister informs colleagues of his or her decisions as a matter of political courtesy and does not expect to be over-ruled by them.

RELATIONS WITH THE EUROPEAN UNION

In those areas of policy which fall within the jurisdiction of the European Union (EU) the Cabinet is not a decision-making body. The EU controls important policies concerning trade, consumer protection, agricultural support, the environment, workers' rights and international transport. Here the key body is the European Council of Ministers upon which Britain is represented by the appropriate Cabinet minister depending on the subject under discussion.

In these circumstances ministers attending important European meetings must clear with prime minister and Cabinet the negotiating line they will be taking before they go. Similarly on their return they must report back on their achievements or their failures. A clear example occurred during 1997 when Labour's new Agriculture Secretary, Jack Cunningham, had to shuttle backwards and forwards to Brussels trying to lift the ban on exports of British beef which resulted from the incidence of BSE in the national herd. The Chancellor of the Exchequer of course faces such diplomacy all the time. He too must keep the Cabinet informed on financial and economic developments.

CABINET COMMITTEES

ORGANISATION

These were introduced under David Lloyd George in 1916. Their importance has grown ever since. A Cabinet committee comprises the following:

A Chairperson	Often the Prime Minister. Otherwise a senior Cabinet minister who is most closely concerned with the subject of the committee's business.
Cabinet Ministers	A small number, perhaps only two or three. When Jack Cunningham was appointed Minister for the Cabinet Office or 'Cabinet co-ordinator' in 1998 he made it clear that he would sit on all major committees. One of the Treasury ministers will also be included where there are large amounts of public expenditure involved.
Junior Ministers	Normally those juniors who have responsibility for the committee's subject.
Senior Civil Servants	Some of the less important committees may include senior civil servants from the relevant departments. Of course such officials are often invited to address a committee or

Invited Witnesses
even full Cabinet, but in only a few cases; normally ad hoc committees where they are permanent members.

Committees may invite outsiders who may be able to give them informed opinion or vital information.

Committees fall into two categories – **standing** and **ad hoc**. Put simply the former are permanent, dealing with areas of policy which *always* concern government. The ad hoc committees are temporary and deal with problems which are expected to be short-term. There are also a small number of sub-committees which enable the work of larger committees to be divided further.

Until John Major took office in 1990 the precise number, functions and membership of Cabinet committees were not published. This is not to say that they were a complete secret. Most members of the political community including journalists knew who made up the key committees and what subjects they were considering. Nevertheless the mystery surrounding them was part of the general culture of secrecy which permeated government until the 1990s. Major determined to let some light into the darker recesses of the governing process and since then the committee system has become a matter of public knowledge.

The committees existing in August 1998 with their responsibilities and chairs are shown below:

Table 3: *Cabinet committees, 6.98*	
STANDING COMMITTEES	
TITLE	CHAIR
Defence and Overseas Policy	Prime Minister
Northern Ireland	Prime Minister
Intelligence Services	Prime Minister
Economic Affairs	Chancellor of the Exchequer
Public Expenditure	Chancellor of the Exchequer
Environment	Deputy Prime Minister
Local Government	Deputy Prime Minister
Home and Social Affairs	Deputy Prime Minister
Queen's Speeches and Future Legislation	Lord Chancellor
Legislation	Leader of House of Commons
Welfare to Work (sub-committee)	Chancellor of the Exchequer
London (sub-committee)	Deputy Prime Minister
Drug Misuse (sub-committee)	Leader of House of Commons
Health Strategy (sub-committee)	Leader of House of Commons
Women's Issues (sub-committee)	Social Security Secretary

AD HOC COMMITTEES	
TITLE	CHAIR
Millenium Date Change	Trade and Industry Secretary
Food Safety	Cabinet Office Secretary
Youth Justice	Home Secretary
Utilities Regulation	Trade and Industry Secretary
Constitutional Reform Policy	Prime Minister
Incorporation of the European Convention	Lord Chancellor
Freedom of Information	Lord Chancellor
House of Lords Reform	Lord Chancellor
Devolution to Scotland, Wales, English Regions	Lord Chancellor
Consultative Committee with Liberal Democrats *	Prime Minister

*This committee uniquely also contains representatives from the Liberal Democrat Party. This is a gesture towards a consensus on constitutional reforms.

RELATIONS WITH CABINET

Much of what the committees decide does not need formal Cabinet approval. The Cabinet Office distributes such decisions to the relevant government departments who then have the task of implementing them. This may involve legislation, amendments to existing legislation, or action by a subordinate public body including local authorities.

In key policy areas, however, Cabinet sanction *is* required. In recent years we can identify a number of such policies which have been considered in committee but which have required a full Cabinet decision:

- Reform of the National Health Service 1988–9
- The replacement of the local Poll Tax by the new Council Tax 1991
- The incorporation of the European Convention on Human Rights into British law 1997 *
- The introduction and level of a national minimum wage in 1998 *.

(* Implementation was later than this date.)

Of course there have been committee recommendations which have had to be referred back by the Cabinet either to the committee or, even further back in the system, to the policy-makers. This happened to the proposals for a Freedom of Information Act in 1998. The Act did not meet with the full approval of the Home Secretary or the Prime Minister and so is to be amended further. Sometimes a whole policy will be withdrawn because Cabinet is unsure of its merits or feels that Parliament will not approve. This happened to Heseltine's attempts to privatise the Post Office in 1993.

The relationship between policy-makers, Cabinet committees and full Cabinet can be summarised in a flow chart shown below:

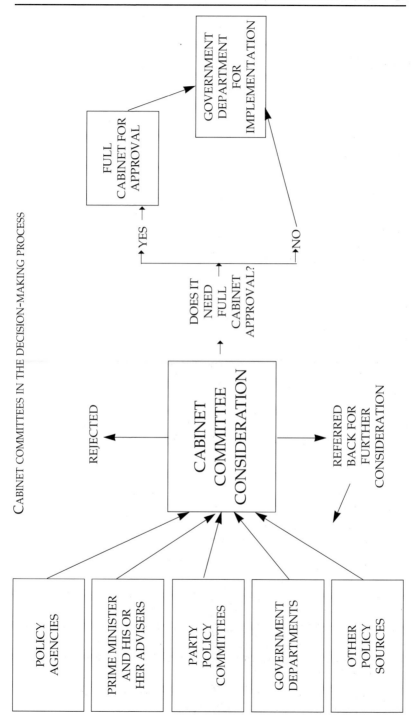

CABINET COMMITTEES IN THE DECISION-MAKING PROCESS

THE PRIME MINISTER AND CABINET COMMITTEES

When Maurice Hankey and Lloyd George introduced Cabinet committees in 1916 it was partly motivated by the heavy workload being placed on the Cabinet and partly by the need to make decision-making more efficient at the centre of government. However, the system was also set up in such a way as to enhance prime-ministerial power. As the committees have grown in number and importance since then, this last phenomenon has become more evident. The committee system extends the influence of the Prime Minister in the following ways:

- The Prime Minister is chairperson of the most important committees (see Table 3 on page 25) and can therefore exercise direct control over policy formulation and the flow of recommendations to full Cabinet.
- The establishment, chair and membership of the committees is in the Prime Minister's hands. This extends his or her powers of *patronage* which is a key element in the wielding of political influence.
- The Prime Minister can ensure that each important committee contains a number of his or her own allies and close supporters so that even in absence representatives can keep an eye on affairs. Blair has used his close friend Lord Irvine for this purpose.

The nature of such prime-ministerial control will be further explored in Chapter 5.

THE CABINET SYSTEM

As we have seen above, it is more meaningful today to think of a Cabinet system rather than merely a Cabinet. This system includes over 2000 individuals whose duties revolve around the Cabinet and its work. They support, supplement and often represent the Cabinet itself. What we can include in this system is fairly arbitrary but it is possible to select the key elements. They can conveniently be divided into five sections:

ADMINISTRATIVE AND POLICY SUPPORT

This is mainly provided by the Cabinet Office headed by the Cabinet Secretary. There are over 2000 civil servants in the office which is conveniently housed behind 10 Downing Street and connects to the Prime Minister's office and the Cabinet rooms. The role of the office and in particular the secretariat section is to ensure that the business of Cabinet and its committees works efficiently. Papers are prepared and distributed, decisions recorded, the flow of information is kept open and the agendas of all the key meetings are drawn up.

The office also processes decisions once they are made. This means informing all those who need and are entitled to know what has been decided. Above all, action may be called for from the law officers (see below), parliamentary managers, the Treasury, and by officials within departments. This is a complex operation and that is why so many officials are involved.

During 1998 the incoming Cabinet secretary, Sir Richard Wilson, recommended a number of reforms to the Cabinet Office. Most of them were accepted and implemented by Tony Blair. When he first re-shuffled his Cabinet in July 1998 he took the opportunity to beef up the policy-making and administrative role of the Office. The principal changes were as follows:

- A senior Cabinet minister, Jack Cunningham, was placed in charge of the Cabinet Office. This considerably enhanced its political authority.
- A number of administrative and policy-making units were added to the Office. These included the:

  Better Regulation Unit to improve the quality of government regulation over business and commerce when this is in the public interest.

  IT Unit and Action 2000 Initiative to deal wiith pressing matters concerning information or computer technology.

  Performance and Innovation Unit whose role is to improve the quality of new policy initiatives. Its first areas of interest were old people, the cities and the regions.

  Centre for Management and Policy Studies to advise central and local government on policy management, and to train senior officials.

  Management Board a team of senior civil servants from different government departments to coordinate policy throughout government.

At the same time a number of key individuals and bodies were incorporated into the Cabinet Office so that their work would be brought closer to the centre of government policy-making. These included the **Women's Unit**, the **Chief Scientific Adviser** and the **Office of Public Service** (which manages the civil service).

These innovations certainly represent a huge advance in the role of the Cabinet Office. However, whether it marks an enhancement in Cabinet power or is designed to increase the pre-eminence of the Prime Minister remains questionable. This issue is considered in Chapter 8.

MANAGEMENT SUPPORT

Every Cabinet committee is shadowed by a so-called **official committee**. These are made up of civil servants. Their role is to gather information and distil options down to simpler choices which ministers in the political committees can handle and digest. In other words they manage the decision-making process.

FINANCIAL ADMINISTRATION

The financial considerations of every decision must be established. Policies must be costed and subsidiary decisions made to decide how the money is to be found. Here the Treasury, its political ministers and civil servants must provide support and constraints. It follows from this that the Treasury (which like the Cabinet Office is located behind Downing Street) is a vital part of the Cabinet system.

LEGAL SERVICES

Most policies and decisions have to be converted into law. A considerable amount of advice is needed therefore from legal authorities. Headed by the Attorney General – a minister though not of Cabinet rank – the legal part of the Cabinet system must help to draw up appropriate legislation and to counsel on the wider implications of decisions. Do existing laws need to be repealed or amended? Will there be any conflict with European Union laws? Do legal pressure groups, the legal profession or the police need to be consulted on the implications? These are all questions which must be asked and answered by the Attorney General and his department.

PARLIAMENTARY MANAGEMENT

We have seen above how decisions coming from the system may have administrative, legal or financial ramifications. But we should not forget that Parliament must be considered. In some cases no legislation is required so that Parliament only needs to be informed In such cases a White Paper, which explains government policy, or a ministerial announcement will be needed. The nature and timing of the information will be handled by the Leader of the House of Commons (a Cabinet minister) and the Leader of the Lords (not in Cabinet). Civil servants may write the papers or announcements, but the arrangements have to be made at high level.

Where actual legislation is required, matters become more complicated. The programme has to be planned carefully, a timetable for debates drawn up and the necessary papers – not least the bill itself – written. In overall control of this planning are the Leaders of the two Houses (though the bills will be drawn up within the relevant department).

But if there is likely to be serious opposition in Parliament – from either House – the Cabinet's business managers must swing into action. Now the whips will be needed to assess the strength of opposition and to determine what action can be taken. In extreme cases the whips may advise that a measure should be dropped, as occurred when legislation to reduce the age of homosexual consent to 16 would not pass through the House of Lords in July 1998 and when Post Office privatisation was dropped in the face of Commons opposition as described above.

In such circumstances the whips become a vital part of the Cabinet system. It must be stressed here that opposition from *other* parties is expected and will not normally thwart legislation as long as the government enjoys a majority in the House of Commons. It is opposition from *within* the governing party which causes problems. The whips must have their ears constantly to the ground and know what MPs are thinking. When trouble does brew it is for them to battle for compliance on behalf of the Cabinet. The House of Lords, which is less predictable but also less influential, must also be nursed through difficult legislation.

INFORMATION MANAGERS

This is an activity which has grown in importance in recent years and has become the most controversial part of the system. It is complicated by the fact that the Prime Minister has his or her own information machine and that every minister and government department also attempts to manage the media and public opinion.

In the heyday of Margaret Thatcher, for instance, it became impossible to distinguish between *her* version of government policy and the official Cabinet line. In the hands of her press secretary, Bernard Ingham, the government's output of decisions was often presented as the Prime Minister's own. Indeed there were occasions when the Ingham version of events differed from the perception of Cabinet members. Certainly Michael Heseltine, then defence secretary, believed this to be the case in the dispute over whether Britain should purchase Westland helicopters in 1985–6. He claimed that the Prime Minister won the argument through the public information system even though the Cabinet backed his view. The dispute was so severe that Heseltine resigned.

John Major enjoyed no such luxury. Leading a Cabinet which was split over Europe there was no one single version of Cabinet policy. The Government Information Service tried to paper over the cracks, but was undermined by rival versions of policy emerging from the press offices of Michael Portillo and Peter Lilley. Major was so incensed that he was famously recorded as having described them as 'bastards' for their treachery.

Tony Blair clearly learned from these problems. Led by Alastair Campbell at the head of the Information Service and Peter Hyman, communications specialist in the Prime Minister's Policy Unit, there is a concerted effort to ensure that only one version of policy comes out of the system. There has developed a veritable industry within government, whose role is to process information. These so-called 'spin doctors' have come in for considerable opposition both from within and outside the Labour Party. Some argue that the *presentation* of policy has become as important as the *substance* of policy itself.

But all governments in the past have managed information to a greater or lesser extent. It is vital for the success of its operations that the Cabinet can feel confident that its output is presented favourably. What *has* changed is the relative importance of this function.

The diagram below indicates how the Cabinet system is organised:

THE CABINET SYSTEM

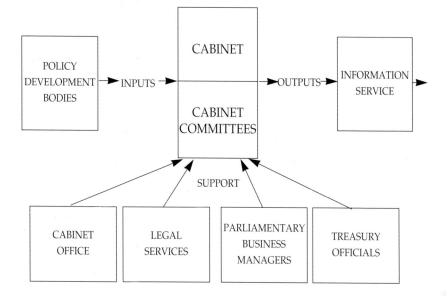

COLLECTIVE CABINET RESPONSIBILITY

The doctrine of collective Cabinet responsibility can be described as follows:

> *All members of the Cabinet must be prepared to support and defend in public any decision which has been formally agreed by the full Cabinet or a Cabinet committee, whether or not that minister privately agrees with the decision. Failure to do so incurs the risk of dismissal from the Government. Any minister who wishes publicly to disagree with a policy so decided must resign from the Government before doing so.*

It would be wrong to assume that this doctrine is unique to politics. It is often a requirement for members of committees in clubs, societies and the like. It is also similar to the constraints which school teachers experience. Not all teachers in a school will agree with all the rules, but they are expected to enforce them for the sake of consistency and good order in the school as a whole. If they do not, they should be prepared to leave the employment of the school.

So it is with government. It requires unity, consistency and singleness of purpose. If it lacks these qualities it is likely to lose public confidence and may even face defeat in Parliament. Where foreign policy is concerned it is especially crucial. Foreign countries can only negotiate with Britain with any confidence if they are sure that the country's representative speaks for the whole government.

The doctrine can be traced back to the very earliest days of Cabinet government under Robert Walpole in the 1720s. He and his successors recognised that the whole idea of having a group of ministers who could run the country collectively, depended upon the maintenance of group discipline. The principle continued to gather strength through to the 1980s.

It has been threatened from time to time, never more so than in 1992–7 when a number of ministers were openly defiant over economic policy and relations with the European Union, but it is still considered to be the key element in the British Constitution. Since 1945 all new Cabinet ministers have been given a version of the rules in a document called *Questions for the Procedure of Ministers* – one of the minority of parts of the Constitution which is clearly written.

Collective responsibility is also now extended to *all* ministers including the 80 or so who are not in Cabinet. It is therefore vital that the decisions of Cabinet and its committees are communicated clearly to the whole government.

It is often now claimed that the principle of collective responsibility has all but disappeared or at least has fallen into disrepute. Whether this is so is examined in the next chapter.

SUMMARY

The main general point to be made is that there is a Cabinet system rather than merely a Cabinet. The main elements of the system include Cabinet committees, the Prime Minister's sources of advice, the newly expanded Cabinet Office and several other institutions which support and advise Cabinet.

It is clear that Cabinet committees play a crucial role. Much business passes through them and to some extent they are decision-making institutions themselves.

The decision-making role of Cabinet itself is very limited. Cabinet has a number of roles and making political decisions is just one of them which rarely comes into play.

What seems to give Cabinet its strength is collective responsibility. Although Cabinet may play a marginal role in the political process at times, its collective strength does maintain unity in the system of government. It is therefore a vital element in rendering British government strong and decisive.

Revision Hints

Notes should be made on the various functions of the Cabinet and the nature and role of Cabinet committees. Students should also be able to place the Cabinet in the wider Cabinet system and in the decision-making process as a whole.

The developments in the position of the Cabinet Office should also be noted. These are some of the most important reforms to be made since 1970.

The other area of interest which should be learned concerns the formation of Cabinets. The factors which a prime minister takes into account should be known and the different styles of Cabinet formation understood.

Exam Hints

Examination questions tend to centre on two areas:

- How Cabinets are formed. What is in the Prime Minister's mind when Cabinet is chosen and what constraints might be experienced in this role. Answers here should take into account both individual qualities of ministers, and factors which determine the make-up of the Cabinet as a whole.
- The importance of Cabinet committees and the development of a Cabinet system, as opposed to merely a Cabinet, may also be examined. Here their functions should be described as well as their relationship to other parts of the governing system.

Practice Questions

1 What factors does a prime minister take into account when appointing his or her Cabinet?
2 What are Cabinet committees? Describe their importance in the political system.
3 Assess the importance of the Cabinet Office in the British system of government.

3

IS CABINET GOVERNMENT
IN DECLINE?

Introduction

THIS CHAPTER OFFERS a critique of modern Cabinet government. In it we examine
the traditional claims which Cabinet can make to being at the heart of the
political system. We look at this from both a constitutional viewpoint – what is
the position in *theory*? – and a political one – what is the current *reality*?

Key Points
- Has the Cabinet become marginalised in the system?
- Is collective responsibility, the 'cement' which holds Cabinet together, in
  terminal decline?
- Has Cabinet government now been replaced by prime-ministerial
  government, as Richard Crossman claimed in 1963?

THE PRINCIPAL ARGUMENTS

The final demise of Cabinet government has been predicted ever since it was
called into serious question by former Labour minister, Richard Crossman in
1963. Though Crossman was mainly concerned with the growth of prime-
ministerial power *at the expense* of the Cabinet, he has since been joined by others
who fear for its future in a number of other senses.

From the huge amount of literature on the subject we can identify FOUR
principal arguments concerning the status of the modern Cabinet:

- The Cabinet with its committees is *still* at the centre of the political process. Though it may *appear* that it is in decline, it remains the crucial institution within the system.
- The real decision-making centre of gravity has irrevocably moved away from the Cabinet system. Its role has in other words become *marginalised*.
- The doctrine of collective Cabinet responsibility and the principle that Cabinet decisions are genuinely collegial have been so eroded in recent times that the original concept of Cabinet government no longer exists.
- The Prime Minister has become so dominant in the political system that the Cabinet system can be controlled to his or her own benefit. In other words it is more accurate to think of *prime-ministerial* government than *cabinet* government.

These propositions are examined below:

CABINET AS CENTRE OF THE GOVERNING PROCESS

We can ask a series of questions of the modern Cabinet, the answers to which may help us to decide whether this argument holds water:

DO CABINET MINISTERS STILL MAKE COLLECTIVE DECISIONS?

The idea of collegiality – that a group of senior ruling politicians do meet together regularly to make important decisions – goes back to the origins of Cabinet in the early eighteenth century. However, it can be suggested that it has never really been a true feature of the system. Of course there have been occasions when reaction to a crisis has to be agreed and the Prime Minister is content for full Cabinet to do this, but it has always been accepted that Cabinet existed as a decision-maker only where the system fails to reach a conclusion *elsewhere*.

In the turbulent 1990s when John Major struggled to present a united government front to Parliament and the media, he did institute the idea of political Cabinets. These were emergency meetings outside the normal timetable and were designed to resolve internal problems among ministers and to determine a common line. The government's attitude to Britain's possible entry into a single European currency system, which was the subject of furious disagreements between Euro-sceptics such as Michael Portillo and Peter Lilley, and pro-Europeans such as Chancellor Kenneth Clark, had to be settled. On occasions like this, collegiality certainly does operate.

What was notable about John Major's troubled administration of 1992–7 was not the fact that the Cabinet was clearly split on a number of issues, but the fact that it *did* stay together for a full term of office even though it lost its parliamentary majority in mid term. This speaks volumes for the ability of Cabinet government at least to give the *impression* of collective government.

The first year or so of Tony Blair's Labour government also suggests that collective decision-making may have been restored. Ministers remain remarkably united on all the important issues; there have been no major resignations over policy and no apparent splits. Though Blair himself presents a presidential *image* there is no suggestion that policy is solely the responsibility of the Prime Minister's office. But we must be careful. We may have been deceived by one of two possible illusions:

- There is a view that the government's information machine, its spin doctors, are so efficient that they have been able to present an *appearance* of collective government even though there are deep divisions.
- A similar idea is that the Prime Minister is dominating the whole system and that collegiality is simply what Crossman called in 1963, 'collective obedience by the whole administration ... to the will of the man at the apex of power.'

Collective government or collective obedience? It is the key question now. Possibly when Blair's government has to get to grips with the more contentious issues such as the single European currency, welfare reform or reform of the electoral system, there will be more clues.

DO ALL IMPORTANT DECISIONS STILL REQUIRE CABINET APPROVAL?

We must first accept that the Cabinet committee system has taken over some of the functions of Cabinet, but this need not invalidate the importance of the Cabinet system as a whole. This said, the answer must emphatically be yes.

The fact that many decisions go through Cabinet or Cabinet committee 'on the nod', that is without discussion, does not mean that Cabinet is impotent. Better evidence are the occasions when the Cabinet or a committee has rejected a proposal whether it has come from the Prime Minister or any other policy-making source. There are plenty of examples. Modern instances of rejected policies have been:

- Frank Field's proposals for reform of the welfare system in 1998.
- Post Office privatisation in 1993.
- Margaret Thatcher's radical proposals to curb trade union power in 1979–80.

So although it is not true to say that Cabinet is the key decision-making body in the system, it remains a final appeal court where policy may be rejected. When they find themselves in broad agreement ministers can over-rule anybody in government.

Some policies have by-passed the Cabinet system as a whole such as Britain's membership of the European Exchange Rate Mechanism and the closure of large numbers of coal mines in the mid 1980s, but it remains true that Cabinet has the *reserve* power to exercise control.

IS IT STILL SEEN AS THE **CONSTITUTIONAL** CENTRE OF POWER?

Again we can give an unequivocal yes here. Despite their modern obsession with the activities of the Prime Minister the media still see the selection of the Cabinet and its toings and froings as the essential activity of government. Similarly when the Prime Minister speaks he or she is always careful to intimate that policy is the output of the Cabinet unless the matter falls under his or her own prerogative powers. In Parliament whenever important announcements are to be made and when weighty debates are held, representatives of the Cabinet line up on the government front bench to demonstrate solidarity.

These phenomena are all indications of the traditional view that we must look to Cabinet if we wish to find the definitive version of official policy.

This is **not** the same as saying that power lies with Cabinet, but rather that it is a **symbol** of ultimate power. There is a legal and constitutional necessity to establish what *is* the government. Cabinet fulfils that role even if decisions were really made elsewhere.

We are left with mixed messages here. There is no doubt that Cabinet is still very important, but whether it merits the description of being at the centre of political power remains an open question.

HAS CABINET BECOME MARGINALISED?

This is not a new issue. As long ago as 1969 Ian Gilmour, later a minister in Margaret Thatcher's first Cabinet, lamented the limited role of Cabinet thus:

> *The tyranny of the deadline, the demands of lunch, the pre-occupation of ministers with the affairs of their own departments, the reluctance of busy men to deal with difficult issues, the gamesmanship of clever ministers in getting their proposals through without discussion, the unwillingness to look ahead or meet trouble until it can no longer be avoided, all conspire to upset the priorities of cabinet government.*
>
> Source: Ian Gilmour, *The Body Politic*, Hutchinson, 1969

To help us with this question as it stands today it may be useful to consider the central decision-making system as a whole. There is no doubt that it has changed radically since 1970. We can first look at the traditional picture and compare that with the current picture:

THE TRADITIONAL SYSTEM

This is relatively straightforward. Policy proposals were developed by one of the following:

- The Prime Minister and a small group of senior colleagues.
- Government departments in the form of its ministers and senior civil servants.
- Party policy committees staffed by MPs.

This limited group of policy formulators would present their proposals to a Cabinet committee or straight to the full Cabinet. They would reject, accept or refer back for more development. Where the Prime Minister wished to maintain control and felt able to do so, the policy would be developed with his or her own advisers and the result presented to Cabinet as a *fait accompli*. Economic policy meanwhile remained in the hands of the Chancellor of the Exchequer, and the Treasury, who usually formed a powerful alliance with the Prime Minister.

THE MODERN PLURALIST SYSTEM

Now proposals may emanate from a plurality of sources. These include:

- The Prime Minister and his or her advisers
- The Prime Minister's Policy Unit
- A small group of senior ministers surrounding the Prime Minister who also wrote the election manifesto
- Key standing Cabinet committees
- External policy agencies favoured by the current government
- Quangos, whose role is policy formulation
- Party policy committees
- Government departments.

As before, foreign and economic policy remain largely in the hands of the Prime Minister, Foreign Secretary and the Chancellor. Other policies are cleared through Cabinet committees. Only when a major dispute arises will the full Cabinet become involved. There is also a vast government organisation whose role is to arrange for the public presentation of policy.

The difference clearly lies in the increased complexity of the modern system. The role of Cabinet is also subtly different. Whereas it was once the practice to clear most domestic policy through the Cabinet, it now appears to be merely a final appeal procedure for inter-ministerial disputes and a final opportunity to coordinate presentation. Cabinet still retains a veto over policy, that is quite certain, but its role has undoubtedly become diluted and therefore less precise.

HAS COLLECTIVE RESPONSIBILITY DECLINED?

Collective Cabinet responsibility is often described as the 'cement' or the 'superglue' which binds British government together. In the sense that it ensures that a government presents a united front to Parliament, the media, the public and the rest of the world, it is a vital component of the efficient secret. We could contrast two opposite circumstances to illustrate this:

Strong Government

A government which cannot be divided publicly, which stands or falls *together* behind its collective policies and which publicly presents a *common* version of its policies

Weak Government

A government where individual ministers openly disagree, where policies may come under attack and then be defended only by *some* ministers while others may join the attack, and where the message to the outside world is blurred or even contradictory.

Of course it has been argued, for example by radical socialist MP and former minister, Tony Benn, that collective responsibility stifles open debate and is fundamentally undemocratic. If ministers disagree in *private* – which nobody denies they do – Benn argues they should be able to express their reservations or outright opposition *openly*. In this way the public will be better informed of the real issues and so be able to make a better judgement on those issues themselves. In other words collective responsibility is part of secret government.

Nevertheless if we agree that Cabinet government equals strong, decisive government then it is certain that efficient operation of collective responsibility is vital to its survival as a principle. Benn's view might well produce more *democratic* government, but it is doubtful whether it would be more effective.

THREATS TO COLLECTIVE RESPONSIBILITY

We can identify three principal developments which might threaten this key doctrine:

- If Britain were to experience *coalition* government in the future where two or more parties share government posts it would be exceedingly difficult to maintain collective solidarity. Politicians who have campaigned on different party manifestos at the previous election would find immense difficulty in changing their public views to satisfy the rules of collective responsibility.
  Though there has not been such a coalition in Britain since 1945, the introduction of a new, more proportional electoral system would increase the possibility.

- The increased use of referenda presents a problem. In 1975 for example, when a split Labour government held a referendum on whether Britain should remain a member of the European Common Market (now the European Union), the doctrine of collective responsibility had to be suspended. Ministers who held strong views *against* British membership had to be 'bought off' during the campaign by being allowed to express their opposition openly. There was a logic to this tactic. If a referendum debate is to be truly democratic, ministers must be freed from their shackles. A decisive yes vote in 1975 restored normality and collective responsibility returned. The ministers opposed to membership had to accept the result or resign.

  There are to be more referenda in the future – notably on Britain's participation in a single European currency and possibly on electoral reform. Should these take place with possibly further campaigns the doctrine of collective responsibility will come under increasing stress.

- Much has been made in recent years of the tightening of the Prime Minister's information machine and ability to impose policies on ministerial colleagues. However, every minister today also possesses an efficient system for disseminating his or her *own* views. Press officers, personal advisers and friendly political journalists have ways of leaking information out to the media and to MPs without technically breaking the principle of collective responsibility. The phrases 'sources close to the Minister suggest …' or 'it is commonly known in Westminster that the Minister …' often mean that a minister has ordered his or her view, which may run counter to official policy, to be made known and has authorised a leak. But technically the rules have not been broken.

  Leaks and innuendoes reached their height in Major's government of 1992–7. Indeed they became so common, and the disguise of unofficial leaks so thinly veiled, that some believed that collective responsibility no longer existed. Under Blair's united government the practice has declined though not disappeared. In the future should a government become excessively divided in private or should prime-ministerial power become overbearing, the potential remains for further evasion of the rule.

So we can make two assertions about collective responsibility today:

1 It still exists in theory and remains a key factor in the operation of the Cabinet system.
2 It has been seriously threatened in the past and may come under renewed strain in the future when new political controversies emerge.

THREAT OF PRIME-MINISTERIAL POWER

Most of the discussion on the relationship between the Prime Minister and the Cabinet system is dealt with in Chapter 6. However, some brief general points can be made at this stage. We can distil the arguments into three contentions:

1   The general contention here stems from an idea that there is a certain finite amount of power existing within government in its broad sense. It follows that if the power of the Prime Minister is indeed increasing as many claim, it *must* be the case that power is being lost elsewhere. If this is so, who is losing the power? Some suggest it is Cabinet and its committees. This has certainly been the argument of Crossman in the 1960s, of Benn in the 1970s and 80s, of a number of former ministers in Thatcher's government and of opponents of Blair's leadership in the 1990s. They say that what was formerly Cabinet government has now become prime-ministerial government.

2   There are others such as George Jones of the London School of Economics (LSE) or academic and journalist Peter Hennessy who suggest that centres of power are always shifting. There may be times when the Prime Minister is dominant and others when he or she is not, and collective Cabinet government is restored. It depends upon a number of factors, which are discussed in Chapter 6.

3   A third possibility is that prime-ministerial power has indeed grown, but not at the expense of Cabinet. Rather it has replaced the influence of individual government departments, party policy committees and of MPs. The role and importance of the Cabinet system has not fundamentally changed. It remains the ultimate arbiter of policy when there is a dispute, it legitimises decisions in whichever part of government they are made, it can deal with urgent crises, its committees are still vital in policy formulation and it can over-rule the Prime Minister if it is determined enough.

SUMMARY

The key points and questions which have been covered in this chapter are as follows:

- There are competing arguments which suggest either that Cabinet is still at the centre of the governing process or that its position has become significantly eroded.
- The idea of Cabinet as a means by which the government reaches *collective* decisions has been called into question.
- There are enormous stresses on the modern Cabinet as a result of the more pluralist nature of decision-making and the extension of resources available to the Prime Minister.
- There is still a debate as to whether British government is better described as *cabinet government* or *prime-ministerial government*.

STUDY GUIDES

Revision Hints

Clear notes should be made on the principal developments which have weakened Cabinet government and those enduring features which still apply today.

The doctrine of collective responsibility must be clearly noted, together with the senses in which it operates and the pressures which have been placed upon it.

The issue of prime-ministerial government should not be tackled at this stage. This should only be attempted in conjunction with Chapter 6. However, at this stage the basic arguments can be noted.

Exam Hints

Exam questions tend to centre upon two issues:

* The nature of collective responsibility, its importance and whether it is in terminal decline. The doctrine must be explained and its importance demonstrated. Examples of its weaknesses should be described and some assessment of future prospects attempted.
* Whether the status, influence and central position of the Cabinet has been so eroded that it is no longer effective. Here the traditional position should be restated and the challenges explained; principally that it has been replaced by prime-ministerial power or that the focus of decision-making has moved elsewhere, leaving Cabinet with only a marginal role.

Practice Questions

1   a   What is meant by the doctrine of collective Cabinet responsibility? Why is it so important?
   b   To what extent does the doctrine still apply?
2   Examine the view that Cabinet is no longer an effective part of the governing process in Britain.

4

THE ROLE OF THE PRIME MINISTER

Introduction

WE TURN TO the office of the Prime Minister as distinct from the Cabinet as a whole. The functions of a modern prime minister are described and discussed. There is also an exposition of the limitations which exist to the impressive list of roles.

The Prime Minister's position is best understood in terms of three principal functions:

- leader of the State (though not strictly head of State, a title reserved to the Monarch)
- head of government
- in nearly all cases, leader of the party which is in government.

The nature of the British polity, which is predominantly a party system, demands that a single party normally wins the general election outright and that the leader of that party should automatically become prime minister.

Key Points
- Policy making and implementation
- Prime Minister as leader of the nation, the government and the party
- Prime Minister as economics manager.

POLICY MAKING AND IMPLEMENTATION

NATURE OF THE ROLE

The business of making government policies and deciding how and when they should be implemented is a complicated affair. It would be an error to believe that even the most dominant of prime ministers such as Margaret Thatcher can make policy alone. In reality policy comes from a variety of sources including the wider party, government departments, a number of policy-making institutions inside and outside government or from Cabinet committees. Indeed when a party comes to power it is largely committed at least for two or three years to its election manifesto commitments.

There have, it is true, been examples of the *personal* interests of a prime minister turning into official policy. The founding of the Open University was Harold Wilson's own project as was John Major's Citizens' Charter. But on the whole, prime ministers do not make policy except as a member of one of the bodies identified above. What they do however, is to influence which policy options should be adopted, what should be the priorities for a government and what should be abandoned altogether. Anthony King, a leading commentator on prime-ministerial power sums the position up thus:

Most British prime ministers are not in the position of having a large number of aims, personal to themselves across a wide range of fields. Their preferences are very much those of their party and the majority of their cabinet colleagues.

Source: Anthony King, in *The British Prime Minister*, Macmillan, 1985

The introduction of the Poll Tax is a good illustration of the Prime Minister's role It was one of a number of options ordered by Margaret Thatcher needed to replace the unsatisfactory system of local taxation. The Poll Tax (she preferred the term 'community charge') was the brainchild of a personal adviser, Lord Rothschild. Once the Prime Minister had made her choice she had to use her authority to ensure that the new policy secured compliance in Cabinet committee and then full Cabinet. The final hurdle, Parliament, proved more tricky and here Thatcher had to call on all her leadership skills to guide the legislation through both Houses.

On the negative side of policy development Tony Blair, barely a year into his premiership, decided to drop the proposals on welfare reform developed by Frank Field and order a fresh review. In order to ensure that he minimised opposition he removed two supporters of the policy from office – Field himself and Harriet Harman.

LIMITATIONS

In both the cases described above we see prime ministers using their considerable influence to promote their own policy preferences. Leaders who are weaker either through circumstances or by inclination may have less choice. Their leadership role must be to determine which policies are likely to attract wide support in Cabinet and the wider party, and then to promote them, sometimes *as though* they were their own programmes. This was certainly the case when John

Major developed the government's policy on a single European currency in 1996–7. James Callaghan too was no great supporter of devolution to Scotland and Wales, but had to lead the government in that direction because it was the only way to preserve a fragile parliamentary majority.

It has long been a complaint of prime ministers that although they are the leading member of their government they have relatively meagre resources at their disposal for policy-making. Some innovations to strengthen the policy-making role of the Prime Minister have been seen – the Central Policy Review Staff in 1971 and Wilson's Policy Unit in 1974 for example – but on the whole it is difficult for even the most able and hard working of prime ministers to devote enough time and expertise to the policy process. Blair is aware of this problem and is in the process of strengthening the Downing Street set-up for the purpose, but he has stopped short of creating a 'prime minister's department'.

One solution to the vacuum in prime-ministerial advice is the practice of setting up special bodies whose role is to report directly to the Prime Minister. Thatcher thus created the Efficiency Unit to modernise the civil service in 1979, and Blair has used the Social Exclusion Unit to advise on various aspects of social policy together with commissions on taxation and electoral reform. But these only tinker with the system. The Prime Minister must still rely on others to develop policy and then must use his or her authority, which varies considerably as we have seen above, to promote the preferred policies.

LEADING THE NATION

There are times in the life of a nation when there is an overwhelming need for unity, or a sense of purpose or courage in the face of a crisis. It is also true that nations should *appear* to be united in their dealings with foreign powers. This applies not just in warfare, but also in international diplomatic or economic affairs. It used to be the case that this sense of national identity could be provided by the Monarchy and in a very limited sense it still can be. But on the whole the British Head of State cannot play such a role. The Monarchy is no longer powerful or respected enough to speak for all the people.

In countries with an elected head of state the President can fulfil this function. How often do we see the American President making momentous pronouncements when the country faces an emergency or a time of great concern? The President is also able to project an image of the country to the rest of the world which is as favourable as possible. But who can do this for Britain? The only answer must be the Prime Minister.

Margaret Thatcher was particularly comfortable in this role. She led the people to war over the Falklands, presented a defiant face to the communist world in the dark days of the Cold War and maintained an uncompromising negotiating position with Britain's European partners. More recently Tony Blair took over the leadership of the national mourning for the death of Diana, Princess of Wales in 1997. In doing so he made an almost direct challenge to the authority of the royal family whose reputation had never been lower than at that time. In 1998 he saw himself as the key peacemaker in Northern Ireland when a political settlement became a real possibility.

But it is not easy for a prime minister to be a truly national leader. In order to be one he or she must put aside party loyalties and attempt to speak for all, no matter what their party affiliations. For directly elected presidents there is less difficulty as they can distinguish between their political and national roles. Prime ministers who owe their authority largely to their party because they are not directly elected by the people may experience a conflict of interests. Thus when John Major was negotiating with the European Union in the mid 1990s he had to weigh up the *national* interest against the fragile unity of his own *party*.

Of course political opponents will always seek to undermine a prime minister as national leader. They may claim, often with justification, that personal political gain is being sought. Fortunately however, it is usually true that a leader who does capture the mood of the nation as a whole will also improve the electoral prospects of his or her party. So in purely *constitutional* terms a prime minister should not be able to represent the nation, but in *practical* terms this is often done.

LEADING THE GOVERNMENT

In the strictest sense this is the official function of the British Prime Minister. This is what he or she has been granted authority to do. The roles as chief policy-maker and as national leader flow from this central function. It can be divided into three aspects – Cabinet controller, head of the bureaucracy, and parliamentary leader.

CABINET CONTROLLER

This position is explored in some depth in the next chapter, but at this stage it is useful to identify what a prime minister is expected to do in relation to the Cabinet. He or she carries out the following operations:

• Appoints, dismisses and transfers all Cabinet members
• Decides what Cabinet committees should be set up
• Determines membership of Cabinet committees
• Either chairs him or herself or appoints chairpersons of committees
• Draws up the Cabinet agenda
• Chairs and controls Cabinet discussions

- Writes minutes of Cabinet meetings thereby identifying decisions
- Settles disputes between Cabinet members
- Establishes inner Cabinets of senior ministers to make key decisions.

Exactly how these functions are used to wield power is discussed below. However, we can say here that this management of Cabinet government has the purpose of maintaining the direction of government while avoiding excessive internal conflict. Of course that direction may be determined by the Prime Minister personally or by the ruling party, or by a general consensus within the government.

MANAGING THE BUREAUCRACY

The Prime Minister is technically head of the civil service. In practice however, most of that role must be delegated to colleagues. He or she may play a leading part in the appointment of the most senior officials (Thatcher was particularly known for interfering in such matters), but is expected to leave it to others to control the civil service. Prime ministers have some officials who report directly to them such as the Cabinet Secretary or those who work in the Cabinet Office and the Prime Minister's office, but most are managed by his or her ministers.

All ministerial department heads are appointed by the Prime Minister and they are often re-shuffled according to their performance or shifting political fortunes. These ministers head a veritable army of bureaucrats and official committees whose role is to implement the work of each government department. Thus most of this aspect of a prime minister's work is totally delegated.

Nevertheless prime ministers do from time to time seek to change the way in which the civil service works. Most significantly Thatcher set up the Efficiency Unit to modernise and streamline the bureaucracy. Both Major and Blair took up her lead and forced through significant reforms. Major introduced the Citizen's Charter to make government more responsive to public needs and more accountable for its performance. Blair is seeking more openness in government and to establish firmer political control over what unelected civil servants do.

Thus although the Prime Minister could not possibly be responsible for the day-to-day running of the government machine, he or she is expected to account for the overall conduct of the government. When the bureaucracy is inefficient, ineffective or even corrupt it is up to the Prime Minister to put things right.

PARLIAMENTARY LEADERSHIP

Whatever the government does, whatever its policies and its programmes it must constantly report to Parliament and account for its actions. Often it is individual ministers who perform this task. They explain what their departments are doing and must respond to criticism and occasional praise. But there are times when the government *as a whole* must be represented in Parliament, the House of Commons in particular. This must be carried out by the Prime Minister.

The most high-profile occasion when we see him or her performing this role is Prime Minister's Question Time (PMQT). This is a 30-minute session every Wednesday in the House of Commons. MPs of all parties have the opportunity to throw any question at the Prime Minister and it is expected that a good account of him or herself and of government's performance will be given. Though in practical terms it has little significance, it is the one time when a large proportion of the electorate see politics at work. It is televised and recorded so that it invariably fills a slot on that day's news bulletins.

The performance of the Prime Minister in Parliament and indeed of his or her opposite numbers in the other parties is an important factor in party morale. It is doubtful whether many votes are at stake as a result of PMQT, but MPs of the governing party do look to their leader for inspiration.

PMQT is a very public occasion, but prime ministers must also regularly address the MPs of their own party. In return for their loyalty they expect to be consulted and informed. Edward Heath lost much authority by forgetting this vital lesson, but Thatcher was especially careful to court her MPs even though she enjoyed comfortable parliamentary majorities. Thatcher summed up the importance of the relationship with MPs in her own account of an address to the Conservative 1922 Committee (the name for all the back-bench Conservatives) in July 1987:

So in an unvarnished speech I told them that they had to take a lot of difficulties on the chin in the last year, but those difficulties had nothing to do with our fundamental approach, which was correct ... I was glad to get warm and noisy applause for this, not simply because I prefer applause to execration, but because such a warm response to such a strong speech meant that the Party was recovering its nerve.

Source: Margaret Thatcher, *The Downing Street Years*, Harper Collins, 1993

LEADING THE PARTY

It is a fixed principle of Britain's uncodified constitution that the Prime Minister should also be the leader of the largest party in the House of Commons. In only exceptional and unusual circumstances would this not be true. Any other situation could certainly not endure for very long. The reason is that we expect the ruling party to be able to control the legislative actions of Parliament. As we have seen above, it is in Walter Bagehot's words part of the 'efficient secret' of the constitution. It follows from this truth that the leader of that party must also be appointed prime minister.

MARGARET THATCHER, THE THEN PRIME MINISTER, SPEAKING AT THE CONSERVATIVE PARTY CONFERENCE IN BRIGHTON, NOVEMBER 1980

Every Conservative Party leader since the Second World War has at some time become prime minister. This is not the case for Labour in the same period. Hugh Gaitskell, Michael Foot, Neil Kinnock and John Smith all failed to gain the highest public office. Nevertheless when either of the main parties elects a new leader it is *in the expectation* that the candidate will one day be prime minister and he or she must therefore have the qualities needed to lead a government, a party and the nation as a whole. He or she should in short be exceptional.

But balancing the roles of prime minister and party leader can be a bed of nails. Labour leaders are especially vulnerable as their party is traditionally less respectful of political authority than are Conservatives. Harold Wilson and James Callaghan both struggled to reconcile the political idealism of party activists with the practicalities of running the government and the country. At times they were forced to cut public expenditure on cherished programmes in health, education and welfare in the interests of good economic management. They also had to abandon programmes when it was clear that a flimsy parliamentary majority threatened the survival of the government.

For Conservatives there is usually less conflict between the two roles. However, there were times when both Margaret Thatcher and John Major had to put their prime-ministerial role before the party. During the economic slump of the early 1980s many members of the Conservative Party were urging Thatcher to abandon her harsh free-market policies and intervene to bring relief to beleaguered industries, just as Edward Heath had done in 1971. Thatcher refused, famously asserting to the annual party conference, 'You turn if you like [a reference to Heath's 1971 U-turn in policy]. This lady's not for turning.' Her determination prevailed. Her authority as prime minister was accepted. Major faced similar opposition over Europe. He too had to tread a precarious line between keeping the party together and doing what he felt was right for the country. In his case however, the price of leading the country into the Maastricht agreement was a divided party and ultimate electoral defeat.

Yet difficult though the fulfilment of both roles may be, all prime ministers must face it. They are of course helped by the fact that when they become prime minister there is an enormous boost to their authority. A mere party leader in opposition enjoys a fraction of the influence of a prime minister. Once in office prime ministers have control of patronage, are free to choose their own front bench ministers and as long as they are supported by the Cabinet can decide which elements of party policy to implement and which to set aside. In other words the ties which the party places round the Prime Minister are loosened and he or she is free to exercise their constitutional powers.

ECONOMIC MANAGER

The task of controlling the economy is one which the Prime Minister shares with the Chancellor of the Exchequer. Where there is a strong alliance between the two it forms an irresistible force. Partnerships such as Blair–Brown, Callaghan–Healey and Heath–Barber have all been able to run the economy with relatively little reference to the rest of the Cabinet.

Yet the *ideological* basis of economic policy is still largely determined by the Prime Minister. The laissez-faire, liberal policies of Thatcher and Heath for example, were imposed upon the Chancellors of the Exchequer concerned. Had they attempted to adopt measures which did not conform to the Prime Minister's vision of how the economy should be run, they would soon have been removed. So the Prime Minister may not control the day-to-day running of the economy, but will certainly seek to maintain general oversight.

Before the 1992 presidential election in the United States one of Bill Clinton's aides is said to have reminded him, 'It's the economy, stupid'. What he meant was that elections are generally won and lost on the state of the national economy and it is a foolish candidate who ignores this truth. This is also usually the case in Britain. A prime minister who did not stress the economic health of the country would indeed be 'stupid'. It is also true that the ruling party looks to its prime minister to play the leading role in securing its re-election every few years. It is therefore the duty of the Prime Minister to deliver a healthy economy for the sake of the party. Loss of control could be fatal. The experience of Thatcher in the late 1980s is instructive.

By the summer of 1989 she had lost the confidence of her chancellor, Nigel Lawson. He accused her of making economic policy over his head using an independent adviser, Professor Alan Walters. The result of the conflict was confusion over policy and the loss of Lawson, who resigned and went to the back benches. Following this split she was defeated by her Cabinet over whether Britain should enter the European Exchange Rate Mechanism. Her loss of control over economic matters was certainly a contributory factor in her fall from power in 1990. These events stand in sharp contrast to the close harmony which prevails between Tony Blair and his chancellor, Gordon Brown. Together they have managed to persuade a sceptical party that tight control over public expenditure was necessary in 1997–8 for the long-term stability of the economy.

Some prime ministers seek to interfere more in economic matters than others. Thatcher certainly could not resist the temptation to pull rank on chancellors and Wilson often involved himself closely whenever an economic emergency loomed up on the horizon. Others such as Callaghan however, recognised that a sound assistant at the Treasury could be trusted to maintain economic control. It is in short a highly variable role.

SUMMARY

Being prime minister is, as we have seen above, a complex business. It involves the holder playing a number of different parts which often conflict with one another. Prime ministers must weigh the interests of the nation as a whole and the success of their government and the electoral prospects of their party against each other. Often they are simply irreconcilable.

But while the multiplicity of his or her roles may cause a prime minister much difficulty, it is also a source of great authority. When one of these roles is going badly he or she may try to revert to success in another area to preserve authority. Margaret Thatcher was a special example of this advantage. She was able to appeal to the people over the heads of the Cabinet or to MPs when her policies were opposed by ministerial colleagues. She knew that the party depended on her, at least until 1990, for its electoral success and that she could bank on her popularity among a sizeable minority of the people when the going got rough in Parliament.

So if we are seeking an ideal model of how to reconcile conflicting roles we should look to Thatcher in her heyday. The Prime Minister who possibly represents the greatest failure in this regard was Edward Heath. Whichever way he turned he found himself unpopular with one of the sources of his authority. He was at times intensely unpopular in the country, suspected by his Cabinet who often felt neglected, or criticised by Conservative MPs for ignoring their views. He did on the whole make a success of controlling the government and was able to introduce important reforms to its organisation. But he was unable to avoid conflict with his other roles.

Revision Hints

As well as building up a comprehensive set of notes on these functions there should also be a complete account of limitations. The difference between the roles of a powerful and a weak prime minister should be noted and a clear view given of the relative policy vacuum which hinders the Prime Minister's ability to engage in policy making. It is especially important to develop a full account of the Prime Minister's relationship with his or her Cabinet.

Exam Hints

Typical questions include accounts of how the role of party leader and prime minister differ. What are the crucial changes which take place? It is possible that questions will require a knowledge of *all* the roles fulfilled by a prime minister – head of party, head of government, Cabinet chairperson and national leader or statesperson. It is important to be able not only to describe these differences but also to make meaningful distinctions between them.

Practice Questions

1 Distinguish between the role of a party leader in opposition and a prime minister in power.
2 Is there any meaningful distinction between the roles of head of state and head of government in Britain?

5

PRIME-MINISTERIAL POWER

Introduction

IN ORDER TO make some sense of the somewhat mysterious nature of prime-ministerial power, this chapter makes a basic division between the *formal* and the *informal* powers attached to the office. In this regard the nature of prerogative powers is examined. This particular feature provides us with an important insight into the origins of prime-ministerial authority. Further sources of prime-ministerial authority are also described and evaluated.

The extent of an individual prime minister's power will vary from time to time. The factors which determine such variations are described. Also included is a description of the constraints which *all* prime minister's must endure. In order to place both these powers and their constraints into context, there is a comparison between the British Prime Minister's status and that of counterparts in France and the USA.

Key Points:
- Formal and informal powers
- Constraints on prime-ministerial power
- Comparisons with France and USA.

NATURE OF POWER

We can usefully divide the sources and nature of prime-ministerial power into two categories – formal and informal powers:

Formal Powers

Powers which are permanent or at least which change only very gradually over time. They have their basis in the British Constitution which, though it is largely unwritten, has virtually the same status as the formal laws of the country. All prime ministers have such powers and have the option of using them to a greater or lesser extent.

Informal Powers

These will vary from one period to another. They will depend upon the short-term political circumstances within which a prime minister operates. They will also vary according to the qualities, character and inclinations of the holder of the office.

Thus for example, it is certain that Margaret Thatcher between 1983 and 1987 had the same *formal* powers as did John Major between 1992 and 1997. However, it is clear that Thatcher enjoyed many more favourable *short-term* circumstances than Major (large parliamentary majorities, a more unified party and weak opposition among several others). Thus she had greater *informal* powers and so was able to appear more dominant.

The nature of these powers can now be examined in detail.

FORMAL POWERS

THE ROYAL PREROGATIVE

The formal powers which are possessed by a British prime minister cannot be explained unless we first understand the nature of the **royal prerogative** or **prerogative powers** as it is also known. In order to do so we must first return to the seventeenth century.

Before 1689 the Monarch enjoyed very wide political powers which were uncontrolled either by Parliament or by the law courts. These powers included:

- Making laws by proclamation
- Waging wars and commanding the army and navy
- Calling elections and dissolving Parliament
- Appointing and dismissing ministers and holders of other public offices
- Creating peers, judges and Church of England bishops
- Taking measures to preserve the security of the state.

This is certainly an impressive list. By contrast the controls which Parliament could exercise over executive power were meagre. Taxation did require parliamentary approval and some legal statutes required its sanction, but there was little else MPs and peers could do other than admonish the Monarch when they disapproved of his or her actions.

Clearly the progress towards democracy which began in earnest in the seventeenth century could not allow this situation to persist. Therefore in a number of stages prerogative powers were eroded. Three steps are worthy of special note:

* The settlement which Parliament made when the Monarchy was restored (the so-called Restoration) after a short republican episode between 1649–60.
* The Bill of Rights of 1689 (not to be confused with the American Bill of 1790) which was agreed when James II was removed from the throne to be replaced by William and Mary.
* The Act of Settlement of 1701 which gave Parliament powers over who was eligible to sit on the throne.

These measures had the effect of whittling away prerogative powers, transferring them to Parliament. Even so a number of these powers were **not** removed. These were of two kinds:

1   Those which concerned the security of the State and its relations with foreign powers – that is command of the armed forces, negotiation of treaties and protection from attempts to undermine the State (today we would call this intelligence work, counter-espionage and anti-terrorist activities).
2   Powers concerned with the operations of government. This included public appointments and dismissals, choosing general election dates, granting honours, and managing the affairs of the Cabinet.

But it was not long before it also became unacceptable for the Monarch to operate these powers even though they had become more limited. At the same time, as we have seen above, some monarchs were not particularly interested in exercising them. So who was to take them over?

It could not be Parliament – it was too large a body and too divided by factionalism. To some extent they were transferred to the Cabinet. But the Cabinet is also not always unified and where the vital interests of the State are concerned political divisions are dangerous. So it had to be the Prime Minister who was becoming the dominant figure in the political system at the same time as the Monarch's authority was declining in the eighteenth and nineteenth centuries.

Now we have our answer. It is a crucial (and to many, rather mysterious) principle of the British political system that prerogative powers are exercised by the Prime Minister alone **on behalf of the Monarch**. But three notes of caution are still required:

1   The *ritual* of allowing the Monarch to *appear* to be making decisions has been preserved. Thus the Prime Minister asks the Monarch to dissolve Parliament

when he or she wishes to call an election. Nobody is under any illusion that the Monarch has a choice, but the tradition is maintained. Similarly when the Prime Minister appoints a colleague as a minister, the new Minister is called to the palace to 'kiss the Queen's hand' as though he or she were her own selection.

2 The Prime Minister can be over-ruled by Cabinet in the exercise of these powers. If the Prime Minister were to attempt to defy a majority in Cabinet they would soon have him or her removed. This was broadly what occurred when Neville Chamberlain was replaced by Winston Churchill in 1940. This phenomenon is further explored on pages 64–7.

3 In the most extreme of circumstances the Monarch could in theory reclaim his or her prerogative powers. If for example, a prime minister was attempting to act in defiance of clear parliamentary and Cabinet opposition, support could be withdrawn by the Monarch. In this case the actions of the Prime Minister would cease to have any legal basis and would not be enforced.

DEFENCE, FOREIGN RELATIONS AND NATIONAL SECURITY

The Prime Minister is commander-in-chief of the armed forces, leads important negotiations with foreign powers, signs treaties on behalf of the nation and presents the international face of Britain to the world. In the most extreme of circumstances he or she must make the final decision to use Britain's nuclear weapons. In countries where there is a politically powerful head of state such as France or Russia this role is performed by the President. But the British Head of State, the Monarch, has no such authority and so the Prime Minister must do it on his or her behalf. Of course there are ministers who share these responsibilities (notably the Defence and Foreign Secretaries) and may indeed take a leading role, but the Prime Minister has ultimate responsibility. Four events from recent history will help to illustrate the nature of these powers:

Falklands War

When Argentine forces occupied the Falklands in 1982, prompt military and diplomatic action was required. While British ministers and diplomats sought a peaceful resolution to the conflict, Margaret Thatcher was exercising her full prerogative powers. She ordered the assembly of a task force to relieve the islands. It was she who decided that full military victory was required and made any key decisions which were needed for the successful conduct of the war. After the war she made a commitment to defending the islands for the foreseeable future. It may have been the military leaders who conducted the conflict on the spot, but there was no doubt that the Prime Minister took all strategic decisions.

Gulf War

In 1990 the United States under the authority of the United Nations put together an alliance of states to liberate Kuwait from occupying Iraqi forces. Britain became the United States' leading ally in the venture. Major had recently been elevated to prime minister and was delighted to be able to initiate his premiership with a foreign triumph. It was therefore an easy decision for him to commit British forces to the Gulf War which followed. The extent of Britain's involvement and the part the country was to play in the post-war settlement lay very much in the hands of the new Prime Minister.

Maastricht Treaty

By 1991–2 the European Union had reached the stage where further integration was inevitable. This was a key stage in Britain's relations with Europe and so the Prime Minister took a personal hand in negotiating the treaty. But Major was to experience problems with his own party in Parliament, and the events surrounding the ratification of the treaty tell us much about the nature of prerogative powers.

There was a majority in the House of Commons against the treaty. This was made up of Labour and Liberal Democrat MPs who supported the *principle* of closer integration, but hoped to embarrass the weak government and dissident Conservative MPs who were opposed to closer union in Europe. Strictly speaking the Prime Minister and the Cabinet did not *need* Parliament's approval. The negotiation and signing of the treaty could have been carried out under *prerogative* powers. Nevertheless Major wanted parliamentary approval. He therefore sought a motion of support in the Commons. By the summer of 1992 however, it was apparent that he might lose such a vote. His authority was thus seriously challenged. Two reactions by the government solved the problem.

On the one hand Douglas Hurd, the Foreign Secretary, told Parliament that Britain would sign the treaty even *without* parliamentary approval. On the other, Prime Minister Major threatened that his whole government would resign and precipitate a general election (which the Conservatives would certainly lose). The combination of threats brought enough Conservative MPs into line for the government to scrape home in the vote on the treaty.

So the principle of prerogative powers was preserved and the authority of the Prime Minister maintained. But the incident also confirmed that there are potential constraints on his or her power.

Good Friday Agreement 1998

Major had made it a personal mission to bring about a lasting political settlement to the problems of Northern Ireland which had caused violent conflict since 1968. He was unable to do so partly because he lacked authority as a leader and – possibly more crucially – he did not enjoy a large enough parliamentary majority to be able to force through change. When Tony Blair took up the challenge after his election in 1997 he had a number of advantages which had been denied to Major.

Although the Northern Ireland Secretary, Mo Mowlem, handled the day-to-day negotiations involved, dealing with the warring factions in the province, it was

Blair in his function as national leader who took up the role of statesperson. He brought together the influence of the Irish Prime Minister, Bertie Ahern, and President Clinton of the USA who were both committed to a settlement. He also stepped in whenever the process towards peace seemed to be faltering. In other words he used his *personal* authority to carry out his responsibility to establish national security.

One further role which a prime minister plays and does so very much alone is control over the intelligence and counter-espionage services. This includes MI5, MI6 and the Special Branch. They all report directly to him or her and take their orders from Number 10. The Prime Minister possesses secret information which nobody else in government has a right to know.

These functions normally fall within the scope of the Head of State – usually an elected president – but since the Monarchy cannot become involved in politics in Britain, it must be taken over by the Prime Minister under prerogative powers.

CABINET MANAGEMENT

We saw in Chapter 1 how the Prime Minister gradually took over control of Cabinet as the Hanoverian Monarchs lost authority during the eighteenth century. Since then the grip exercised by prime ministers has tightened. The relationship between a prime minister and his or her Cabinet is both complex and variable. However, we need to establish a number of fixed principles in this central aspect of British government. The Prime Minister:

- alone appoints or dismisses Cabinet ministers and may move them from one department to another (if they agree).
- decides what Cabinet committees shall be formed, who will chair them and who shall be members.
- determines the agenda of the Cabinet while those of committees are also heavily influenced by him or her.
- chairs meetings of Cabinet, summing up discussions and announcing what has been decided. He or she also guides the Cabinet Secretary in the writing of the minutes which are used to inform others of decisions reached. If there is any doubt as to what decision has been reached the Prime Minister clarifies the picture.
- may call emergency Cabinet meetings including partial gatherings where not all members are invited.

But these are only the bare bones of the situation. The true nature of the relationship between a prime minister and his Cabinet is less clear. This is discussed in more detail in Chapter 6. Nevertheless the *formal* powers are possessed equally by all prime ministers.

PATRONAGE

Several thousand posts in public service are in the hands of the Prime Minister. Obviously he does not *literally* appoint them all, but does have the option of exercising influence or of vetoing a decision made by a colleague. Of course, the most senior positions – the Cabinet, junior ministers etc – are directly the result of his or her own decisions. The list below identifies most of the posts over which the Prime Minister has direct or indirect control:

- Cabinet ministers
- Peers
- Junior ministers
- Senior civil servants
- Archbishops and bishops of the Church of England
- Heads and members of other public bodies
- Senior judges
- Knighthoods and other honours
- Heads of public corporations.

Patronage is naturally a power in itself. But it also serves to enhance the influence of a prime minister. Those appointed owe him or her a debt of gratitude and even loyalty. He or she can therefore expect some degree of political support from them (but may not always get it of course). The main exception to this principle is the power to appoint judges. In political cases they are certainly required to be impartial.

DISSOLUTION

It is the law that there must be a general election within five years of the last election. However, there are two circumstances where an election may take place before that maximum period. One is when there is a vote of no confidence in the government passed in the House of Commons. The Prime Minister can do nothing about this unwritten convention. James Callaghan's government suffered such a fate in March 1979. The other situation is when the Prime Minister decides to dissolve Parliament and call an election earlier than legally necessary.

The power of dissolution gives a prime minister two additional strengths:

Firstly he or she can time the election to give maximum advantage to the government, in other words when there are favourable political circumstances for the ruling party. This certainly lay behind Thatcher's early election in 1987 following an economic boom. It can however, backfire. A case can be made for suggesting that four recent prime ministers misused this power with disastrous effects. Harold Wilson (too early in 1970) and Edward Heath (misjudged in 1974) both lost elections they expected to win. Callaghan in 1978–9 and Major in 1994–5 delayed elections fatally. They both went nearly full term and probably did worse than they might have done had they gone to the country earlier. This power may indeed be a poisoned chalice.

Secondly prime ministers may use it as a threat against their own party. Especially when the government has a narrow majority in the House of Commons, a back-bench revolt might spell a no confidence vote and the government would fall. In order to head off such revolts therefore the Prime Minister may simply threaten to resign the government, dissolve Parliament and so precipitate an election. MPs do not like fighting elections especially when there is a danger that they may lose their seat. Similarly MPs prefer their party to be in power. An election might result in a government defeat which such MPs would not want. This threat therefore is a useful device to maintain party discipline on the backbenches. Callaghan used it by implication during his minority government in 1976–9, and Major used it explicitly in 1992 to force through the Maastricht Treaty.

Use of the power of dissolution may well become a game of bluff and counter-bluff. It is also, as we have seen, a dangerous game for prime ministers to play. Yet despite calls to get rid of it by introducing fixed terms for Parliament, party leaders are reluctant to see it abolished.

INFORMAL POWERS

POLITICAL AUTHORITY

Power and its weaker version, influence, have to be distinguished in democratic politics from political authority. The term 'authority' is quite difficult to define, but we can usefully adopt a description offered by Robert Stradling:

Getting others to support you and/or agree with you because they respect you or because they believe you have superior knowledge or because they believe you have the right to make decisions for them.
Source: Robert Stradling, in *Political Education and Political Literacy*, Longman, 1978

So a prime minister is able to exercise personal power *because* a certain amount of *authority* has been granted, as defined above, that is people in the political system believe he or she is broadly right or is worthy of respect, or because the Prime Minister has been given the right to make decisions. Where does authority come from? The answer is that it flows from a number of sources. Indeed it is the very fact that a British prime minister has several sources of authority that he or she enjoys so much potential power. The sources are as follows:

The Monarch

As we have seen above, the Monarch delegates all prerogative powers to the Prime Minister.

The people

Although, unlike a president, the Prime Minister is not *directly* elected by the people, there is no doubt that the fortunes of a party at elections rely to some extent on the personal popularity of its leader – the prospective Prime Minister. Who can deny for example, that John Major's personal qualities were largely responsible for the surprise Conservative victory in the 1992 election? Conversely a prime minister who loses the respect of the people cannot survive for long. Heath discovered that in 1974.

The ruling party

It is virtually always true that the British Prime Minister is leader of the party which can command a majority in the House of Commons (Churchill was a brief exception to this rule). Therefore as long as the party supports its leader when in government he or she can claim to be exercising the authority granted by the party which won the last election.

Parliament

Although, strictly speaking, Parliament cannot remove a prime minister it is certainly true that a prime minister can no longer exercise power if he or she loses the support of a majority in the House of Commons (the respect of the House of Lords is less critical). Major had reached this point in 1996–7 and so became something of a 'lame duck' prime minister in the last days of his doomed Conservative government. But a prime minister who is able control the majority in the House of Commons – one of Thatcher's greatest skills – can enhance his or her powers considerably.

The Cabinet

In the role of Cabinet chairperson the Prime Minister has certainly been given the authority to settle disputes between members of the Cabinet and to control their discussions. The Latin term, *'primus inter pares'* (first among equals) expresses this well. They can over-rule the Prime Minister but on the whole they allow him or her to speak on their behalf. Furthermore the doctrine of collective Cabinet responsibility means that no member of the Cabinet may contradict the Prime Minister's version of policy without risking dismissal. When a prime minister speaks he or she enjoys the *collective authority* of the Cabinet.

Other sources

The wide powers of patronage which a prime minister enjoys are described on page 60. Those who have been thus appointed to senior public office may feel they owe a debt of obligation to the Prime Minister. This represents a further source of authority. They are likely to respect the individual who has elevated them to high office. This may apply to senior civil servants and the heads of a wide variety of quangos and other public bodies.

The way in which political authority is converted into political power is shown in the diagram below.

THE PRIME MINISTER'S AUTHORITY AND POWER

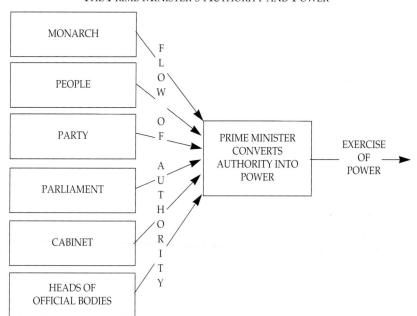

We must now examine the circumstances which will affect both how much authority is granted a prime minister and how effectively he or she is able to convert authority into power.

FACTORS AFFECTING POLITICAL AUTHORITY

The formal, largely prerogative powers, which are discussed on pages 55–61, are largely permanent. The informal powers of the Prime Minister do however, vary considerably. As a guide we can identify the principal factors which will determine how much informal power a prime minister is likely to enjoy. These are shown in the table below:

Table 4: *Short-term factors enhancing informal powers*	
FAVOURABLE FACTORS	PROMINENT EXAMPLES
Large parliamentary majority	Thatcher 1983–90
Good media image	Blair
Dominant personality	Thatcher
Cabinet control	Callaghan
Personal popularity	Blair
United party	Blair
No major ideological splits	Blair
Healthy economy	Wilson 1966–8
International prestige	Thatcher, Blair
No serious leadership rivals	Callaghan, Blair
Extensive use of patronage	Thatcher, Wilson

Clearly when the converse of these advantages prevail, a prime minister will lose short-term influence and will have to rely upon formal powers alone.

The more advantages a prime minister can 'collect', as though he or she were playing a family board game, the more likely he or she is to be able to exercise extensive influence. From the list shown in the table above, it appears that Thatcher and Blair score the highest points. On the whole, events appear to have borne out such an analysis.

Tony Blair and Margaret Thatcher may have accumulated an impressive set of favourable circumstances to enhance their leadership, but all prime ministers experience constraints on their influence. These are also variable as we shall see below.

CONSTRAINTS ON PRIME-MINISTERIAL POWER

The factors which will restrain the power of the Prime Minister have their origins in the same locations which give rise to authority. The only realistic exception is the Monarchy. Only in the most extreme and unlikely circumstances would a monarch intervene to thwart the actions of a prime minister. It is *theoretically* possible but we may safely dismiss it here. We should therefore start with public opinion.

PUBLIC OPINION

Prime ministers do not *have* to listen to public opinion. Nor do they worry overly about their personal ratings in opinion polls. There have indeed been times when prime ministers have been exceedingly unpopular. Thatcher for example, had a satisfaction rating which never reached 50% and which dropped in the early 1980s as low as 29%. Heath, Wilson and Major also endured periods of unpopularity.

Nevertheless the public standing of a prime minister does have some influence on attitudes in Parliament or among voters at election time. Political parties certainly become uneasy when their leader does not have popular respect, as elections – both national and local – are looming. This was certainly one of the factors in the Conservative Party's decision to oust Thatcher in 1990. As long ago as 1964–5, too, the Conservatives became alarmed at the low public standing of their leader, Sir Alec Douglas-Home. They had no hesitation therefore in replacing him with Heath in 1965 before too much damage was done.

Does this mean that prime ministers are constrained by public opinion? The answer is probably, to a limited extent. Leaders are generally more concerned about their standing with the party, Parliament and Cabinet.

THE RULING PARTY

It used to be a common assertion that a Labour prime minister was more constrained by his or her party than a Conservative counterpart. To a great extent however, this position has been reversed in the late 1980s and 1990s.

From the mid 1980s onwards the influence of the unions and grass-roots membership of the Labour Party over their leader have been gradually eroded. The National Executive Committee of the party – its elected leadership group – lost much of its influence over policy, especially the election manifesto. The annual conference, where all party members are represented, used to call leaders to account whether or not they were in government. Wilson and Callaghan certainly found themselves in some difficulty, mainly over economic, industrial relations and nuclear policy, with the wider party. Reforms in the party structure and organisation under three successive leaders – Kinnock, Smith and Blair – have however, considerably enhanced the position of the leader.

The Conservatives have always been seen as a 'top down party' where the authority of the leader was rarely challenged especially when he or she was also prime minister. But under Thatcher the 1922 Committee, which comprises all back-bench Conservative MPs, began to flex its muscles on a regular basis. She was able to control it, but her successor, Major, was constantly called to account by the backbenchers notably over European policy. The wider membership too has also forced the leadership to move towards more nationalistic and authoritarian policies.

So once again we may say that the party membership must be listened to, but this should not be exaggerated. If a prime minister of either major party is determined enough to defy the party he or she usually possesses enough weapons to prevail.

PARLIAMENT

Despite the invariable loyalty which MPs tend to show for their leader it is also true that prime ministers must always carry their backbenchers with them if they are to force through any policy which is likely to be controversial. Occasionally prime ministers have been thwarted by Parliament, for example when Wilson unsuccessfully attempted to reform industrial relations in 1968–9. It also sometimes happens that MPs can insist upon amendments to legislation in return for compliance.

Yet prime ministers with a comfortable majority need not worry too much about the reaction of MPs to their plans, or the conduct of their leadership. At Prime Minister's Question Time every Wednesday the number of hostile questions for Tony Blair from his *own* party is very small. Of course the opposition will give the Prime Minister a hard time but in the final analysis this is only 'window dressing'. The authority of the Prime Minister is rarely seriously challenged in the Commons. Indeed, leaders with large parliamentary majorities such as Thatcher and Blair have experienced more obstruction from the Lords than the Commons!

With a precarious majority in the Commons the position does change. Callaghan and Major in particular were forced to consider the views of their own back-benchers when formulating policy. As we have seen above, Major's dealings with the European Union were virtually dictated to him by the attitude of a group of dissident MPs who threatened to bring his government down at any time. Callaghan in 1978–9 faced a similar set of circumstances. The constraint exercised by Parliament is therefore usually limited but, above all, depends upon the size of the government's majority.

THE CABINET

This is undoubtedly where the power of a prime minister is principally controlled. Though the Cabinet rarely votes in the strict sense of the word, a prime minister can do little if there is a determined majority against him or her in Cabinet on a major issue. Even Margaret Thatcher, who was famed for her ability to ignore colleagues, was occasionally defied by her Cabinet. In the early 1980s before she had gained full control, her proposals for privatisation and industrial relations reform were certainly restrained by senior colleagues. Later too she had to bow to Cabinet pressure to join the European Exchange Rate Mechanism (ERM) in October 1990 against her better instincts.

In reality prime ministers do not bring to Cabinet any of their policies unless they have already ensured that it will be endorsed by ministers. So the constraints exercised by Cabinet tend to be informal. The fact that prime ministers rarely experience defeats is because they have already assessed the likely opposition. The early indications are that Tony Blair is proving to be the most effective manager of Cabinet opinion. He has used Cabinet co-ordinators – Peter Mandelson and then Jack Cunningham – to secure approval for key policies or to recommend manoeuvres which are designed to reduce hostility. Whether this apparent weakening of Cabinet control becomes permanent remains to be seen.

COMPARISONS

The constraints which have been described above are of a relatively informal nature. If we add more formal factors we can build up a picture of prime-ministerial power which can be compared with other political systems. The table below shows the position of the British Head of Government in comparison with counterparts in the USA and France.

Table 5: *Comparison in the exercise of power by heads of government between three political systems*			
ROLE	BRITAIN	USA	FRANCE
Party leadership	Normally dominates a single, strong, unified party	Leads a disunited, loose party structure	Often leads a less stable coalition of more than one party
Patronage	Has complete control over all senior appointments	Senior appointments require congressional approval	Shares patronage with president. Choice of cabinet needs parliamentary approval
Choice of election date	Free choice by prime minister	Fixed terms	Fixed terms
Control of cabinet	Mostly in control but can be outvoted	Controls completely	Limited control. Parties also exercise influence
Control of legislature	Uses leadership of majority party to control Parliament	Very limited	Controls majority but can be fragile especially with coalition government
Foreign policy control	Pre-eminent	Pre-eminent. Some congressional limits over war and treaty-making	Little power. Mostly controlled by the President
Spokesperson for government	Role dominated by prime minister	Dominated by president	Role shared between prime minister and president
Notes: In the USA the President is head of government as well as head of state In France the Prime Minister shares power with an elected president In Britain the Monarch is head of state but has no political power.			

We can see clearly that the British leader has great advantages over the others. In terms of foreign policy his or her role is rivalled by the American President, but where domestic policy is concerned the British Prime Minister enjoys an exceptionally dominant position.

SUMMARY

This chapter has demonstrated that prime-ministerial power is neither simple, nor is it constant. It is important to distinguish between those powers which are formal and permanent, applying to all prime ministers, and those which are informal and are far from reliable. The political circumstances within which a prime minister must operate affect very significantly the amount of informal power which is available. Sometimes the changing circumstances may be controllable, but very often a prime minister must simply accept the inherited political environment.

It must also be carefully noted that there are always important constraints to prime-ministerial power. Though British government has an international reputation for being heavily centralised, there remain strong forces which can restrain central executive control. These include parliamentary sovereignty and collective Cabinet government.

STUDY GUIDES

Revision Hints

The two most important headings under which notes should be taken are (a) to distinguish between short-term and long-term circumstances under which a prime minister exercises power and (b) the contrast between the extensive powers of the Prime Minister (both short and long-term) and the constraints to that power. Appropriate comparisons between the British head of government and counterparts in France and the USA should be noted to illustrate these points.

Exam Hints

It is particularly important to identify distinctions and similarities between features of the Prime Minister and a president. In examinations the American President is most useful as a point of comparison.

Examiners also frequently ask questions about the distinction between the *constitutional*, permanent, formal powers of the Prime Minister and his or her *political*, short term, informal powers. This material should be seen in conjunction with the information in Chapter 6 (b) below.

Practice Questions

1   What limitations exist in the exercise of prime-ministerial powers?
2   Distinguish between the powers of a British Prime Minister and those of an elected president.
3   What (a) short and (b) long-term circumstances affect the powers of the British Prime Minister?

6

PRIME-MINISTERIAL OR PRESIDENTIAL GOVERNMENT?

Introduction

THIS CHAPTER BEGINS by re-examining the perennial question about the centre of British government – has it now become prime ministerial in nature? A variety of views on this subject is described. A similar, though crucially different question concerns the claim that the British Prime Minister is now almost indistinguishable from a United States president. There is a full assessment of the range of issues in this area of enquiry.

There is also a description of the concept of spatial leadership which can now be applied to the heads of government in both Britain and the United States. We therefore examine this idea of spatial leadership as it pertains on both sides of the Atlantic. Finally we examine the argument that the office of Prime Minister has indeed become a *kind* of president, but that this is of a peculiarly British character.

Key Points:
- The meaning of prime-ministerial government
- Prime Minister or president?
- Assessment of prime-ministerial power today.

MEANING OF PRIME-MINISTERIAL GOVERNMENT

This concept cannot be described in one single passage. It has had a long history and has taken many forms. Some of the most prominent arguments are described below.

BYRUM CARTER

The discussion of whether Britain now has prime-ministerial government is usually traced back to 1963 when Richard Crossman, a future Cabinet minister under Harold Wilson, wrote an introduction to a new edition of Walter Bagehot's *The English Constitution*. Though this proved to be a key work on the subject, it was by no means the first time that the increasing power of the Prime Minister had been noticed.

As long ago as 1955 the American analyst Byrum Carter was discussing such changes. Writing at the end of the ailing Winston Churchill's premiership he commented:

The Prime Minister is much more than 'primus inter pares'. The change from the status of Cabinet Minister to the position of Prime Minister is not merely a change of place but a change of dimension.

Source: Byrum C. Carter, *The Office of Prime Minister*, Faber & Faber, 1955

Byrum Carter suggested two principal reasons for the growth of prime-ministerial influence. One was the experience of the Second World War when Churchill had claimed almost dictatorial powers, some of which had been retained during peacetime. The potential power of the Prime Minister had been discovered and it was difficult to put it away. Secondly he identified the vastly increased role of the State which took place during the Labour reforms of 1945–51. This made it more essential to allow a single figure, the Prime Minister, to oversee the process of change.

RICHARD CROSSMAN

Eight years later Crossman had been influenced by the experience of Harold Macmillan's period in office. Macmillan had used his patronage powers extensively to elevate himself to an unprecedented level of authority. In 1962 indeed he had dismissed one third of his Cabinet on the so-called 'Night of the Long Knives' (a reference to Hitler's purge of the German Nazi Party in 1933). Macmillan had also taken to running British foreign policy almost single-handedly and enjoyed a remarkable degree of attention from the press and the newly popular television.

Richard Crossman's words have become part of the accepted mythology of British government:

The post-war epoch has seen the final transformation of cabinet government into prime-ministerial government.

Source: Richard Crossman, *Introduction to the English Constitution*, Fontana, 1963

He went on to add that the *appearance* of collective Cabinet government had been maintained but that this was an illusion. The Cabinet had indeed become only a formalised, 'dignified' part of the political system. Thus it may *appear* that Cabinet is making decisions, but in truth it is merely ratifying policies made elsewhere – mainly in the Prime Minister's office.

TONY BENN

A long serving Cabinet minister and veteran leftwinger in the Labour Party, Benn has long warned against the growing power of the holder of the office of prime minister. He takes a more radical position than Carter or Crossman and suggests that British democracy itself is threatened by prime-ministerial government. While Crossman was more concerned about the weakening of Cabinet control, Benn saw dangers for every aspect of the political system. He is vehement in his criticism of developments:

> *The present centralisation of power into the hands of one person has gone too far and amounts to a system of personal rule in the very heart of our parliamentary democracy.*
> Source: Tony Benn (1979), quoted in *The British Prime Minister*, Anthony King (ed.), Macmillan, 1985

In particular he asserted that there were insufficient democratic controls from Cabinet, Parliament or the political parties over the modern Prime Minister. His solution was to create what he called a 'constitutional premiership' where the powers of a prime minister would have been carefully limited by constitutional principles.

THE THATCHER EXPERIENCE

The debate over the growth of prime-ministerial government gathered pace in the Thatcher years from 1979–90. Former Cabinet ministers who had been dismissed by her or had simply felt it necessary to resign queued up to complain in their political memoirs that she had hijacked government and had subverted Cabinet authority. Among them were the dismissed James Prior and Ian Gilmour, and the disaffected Michael Heseltine, Geoffrey Howe and Nigel Lawson.

But their evidence is potentially flawed. They had, after all, fallen out with her either personally or politically. Small wonder then that they should claim that she had over-used her powers. It is also true that a long serving prime minister is bound to make as many enemies as friends. Furthermore there are also plenty of her allies who will protest that she used the Cabinet a good deal and only exercised her considerable authority when it was absolutely necessary; mainly when there was a political impasse which needed a drastic solution. Dennis Kavanagh has implied this by suggesting that it was Thatcher's personality which was most striking and not any permanent change to the nature of the office:

Mrs Thatcher's success as a Prime Minister illustrates the importance of the office-holder's personality rather than institutional change.
Source: *Social Studies Review*, Vol. 6, No. 4, March 1991

As her years in power came to an end and when she was succeeded by John Major, who promised to restore collective government, the belief that Thatcher had radically changed the nature of the office receded. Nevertheless it is an hypothesis which remains popular and has been revived under Tony Blair.

SUMMARY

Having considered some of the leading views on the subject of prime-ministerial government we need to summarise what the term has been used to mean. The following beliefs and/or developments are important:

- There has been gradual weakening of the collective authority of the Cabinet. It has largely been replaced by prime-ministerial power.
- The increasing grip which political parties exercise over parliament has strengthened the hand of successive prime ministers since they are leaders of these parties.
- The growing importance of the media in politics has meant that government increasingly needs a dominant figure who can represent it. The media themselves tend to prefer to focus upon a single individual.
- There has been a steady increase in the availability of policy advice for the Prime Minister. This has enabled him or her to rival the influence of ministerial colleagues.
- The scope of patronage which the Prime Minister can exercise has increased. In particular there are more quangos and other public bodies whose membership is heavily influenced or controlled by the Prime Minister

There is no doubt that the above changes have seen a growth in prime-ministerial power. Whether or not this represents a *permanent* trend and whether it constitutes a fundamental shift in the balance of power within government are still open to question.

IS THE PRIME MINISTER NOW A PRESIDENT?

We need to be careful here to define what is meant by the term 'presidential' as opposed to the idea of 'prime-ministerial ' government. The following features of the position of a president must be stressed. For this purpose we should use the American model since it represents probably the most powerful example of this kind of head of state.

A DISPLAY OF UNITY: BRITISH PRIME MINISTER TONY BLAIR AND US PRESIDENT BILL CLINTON
DURING A JOINT PRESS CONFERENCE IN FEBRUARY 1998

PRESIDENTIAL STRENGTHS (USA)

The President:

- is elected directly by the people. Authority is therefore drawn from the people
- does not depend upon the constant support of the legislature to survive in office. The President can afford to be defeated in Congress sometimes quite frequently, without feeling the need to resign and is expected to negotiate with the legislature rather than dominate it.
- is head of state as well as head of government and can therefore play one role off against the other. He or she may for example appeal over the heads of the party and the legislature to the people who elected him or her and on whom the President depends for re-election.
- can with full justification claim to represent the nation as a whole while other government leaders are seen as partisan politicians who operate in the interests only of their own party.
- has enormous patronage. Perhaps 4,000 officials are appointed by the President at the start of the administration. The President also has a free hand in the appointment of Cabinet and is not especially constrained by the wishes of his or her party.
- has at his disposal an enormous bureaucracy which turns him or her into the head of a veritable policy-making empire.

- has very direct access to the media and can speak both to and for the nation when he demands it.

PRESIDENTIAL LIMITATIONS

For all the impressive powers described above, it would be a mistake to see a president as all-powerful. There are also constraints which create firm limitations on his or her position.

- The USA like most modern democracies has a strict constitutional framework. The role and powers of a president are therefore limited by constitutional rules which simply cannot be ignored.
- There is a system of checks and balances in place whereby other institutions are able to act as a control mechanism against presidential power. Thus although Congress finds it very difficult to remove a president it may defy his or her political initiatives with enthusiasm. The Supreme Court too can thwart the plans of a radical president as Franklin D. Roosevelt found to his cost.
- The existence of a fixed term of office (four years) means that the President does not have the power to choose the most favourable time to fight a re-election battle.

PRIME MINISTER AND PRESIDENT

On the whole it is clear that the British Prime Minister does not conform very closely to the model which is described above. It *is* true that there are similarities in *style* between the two offices, and it *is* true that Prime Ministers have developed powers and a larger apparatus which begin to look like the presidential circumstance. He or she does have more patronage, does have more policy-making back-up than in the past and can if skilful enough , manipulate the media. But the remaining differences still seem to outweigh the similarities. This can be shown by the table below:

Table 6: *Comparison of Prime Ministers and Presidents*	
SIMILARITIES	DIFFERENCES
• More patronage	• President is also head of state
• Better use of media	• President has authority directly from the people
• More policy-making support	• President cannot be removed by the legislature except for misconduct
• Tendency to appear to be a national leader	• President's popularity does not depend on support for his or her party
	• President suffers in-built political checks
	• President operates within constitutional constraints

So we can see that there remain important differences, some of which cannot in the foreseeable future be altered.

One solution to the problem of whether the British Prime Minister is becoming effectively a president has been offered by Michael Foley in his ground-breaking work *The Rise of the British Presidency* (MUP, 1993). Foley suggests that something fundamental has happened to the office of prime minister, but it does not constitute a move towards the American model. The centre of his theory he calls *spatial leadership*.

SPATIAL LEADERSHIP

Michael Foley has noticed that there was a tendency among American presidents to distance themselves from the activity of government while still remaining dominant within the political system. In other words they made themselves deliberately into *outsiders*.

The most important example in modern times was Ronald Reagan (1981–9). Reagan was a rightwing Republican who was deeply suspicious of government and believed that much of what went on in Washington acted against the interests of the people. As he is quoted by Foley:

Government is not the solution to our problems. Government is the problem.

By remaining outside the main system Reagan was able to disassociate himself from unpopular policies proposed by Congress and at the same time to criticise them when he wished. He could do this because he had been able to gather a wide constituency of support for his *personal* leadership. When he wished to exert his authority over the political system he could use his presidential powers added to popular support. He became a *populist* leader. This meant he recognised not only those policies which appealed to a consensus in the country and which he pursued, but also policies supported only by a minority and which he could therefore attack.

Michael Foley sums up the concept of spatial leadership in the American context thus:

This [spatial leadership] refers to the way that recent presidents have sought to enhance their position in Washington by creating as much distance between them and the presidency ... The strategy allows a president to remain an integral and even a central part of government whilst at the same time affording him the opportunity of detaching himself from government.
Source: Michael Foley, *The Rise of the British Presidency*, MUP, 1993

Though he concentrates on Reagan, Foley suggests that this tendency applies to presidents before and since the 1980s.

He then proposes that this is also happening in Britain. Here the key personality was Margaret Thatcher.

SPATIAL LEADERSHIP IN BRITAIN

Margaret Thatcher was certainly an outsider. A number of factors can be identified in this respect:

- She was a woman in a man's world. The Conservative Party probably only elected her on the basis that she was a caretaker who would soon give way to a permanent choice nearer to the 1979 election. In the event she survived and won that election. As time passed the shock of being led by a woman waned, but it is still true that she needed to be especially dominant in order to counteract some gender prejudice.
- She had a strong ideological commitment to a new set of 'New Right' doctrines. This alienated many traditional Conservatives who believed that politics should be pragmatic rather than principled.
- Her individual dominance set her apart from her colleagues. She was less interested in collective government than in the implementation of her own ideas.
- She was extremely suspicious of many aspects of government. She saw the civil service as wasteful and undynamic. The Cabinet was a frustrating constraint and local government was a threat to her dominance over policy-making.

All in all therefore her performance in government was remarkably similar to that of Ronald Reagan. It is no coincidence that they became great friends and allies. Just as Reagan had expressed the American people's traditional suspicion of government she enjoyed her role as the individual fighting against ineffective colleagues. Foley describes her view as follows:

'I am the cabinet rebel', she once remarked with pride. It was important to her personally to be a rebel. But it was even more important for her political position and leadership style to be seen as a rebel.

Source: Michael Foley, *The Rise of the British Presidency*, MUP, 1993

John Major appeared at first sight to be a more conventional prime minister. He claimed that he would restore collective government and he could often seem self-effacing. After his election victory in 1992 he felt able to adopt a more independent position. He stood above his warring Cabinet colleagues and was even prepared to risk his own position to assert his leadership.

Like Thatcher, he came to believe that low quality government was one of Britain's greatest problems. The Citizens' Charter, which required state-run organisations to be more responsive to public demands, was his own project and formed his response to the low opinion he had of the public sector. So he too became an outsider in his own government. He was certainly consistently more popular in the opinion polls than the rest of the government. He knew he had won the 1992 election almost single-handedly and understood that divisions in the Cabinet were liable to spell the downfall of the Conservative Party in the future.

ASSESSMENT OF PRIME-MINISTERIAL POWER TODAY

The debate over prime-ministerial power continues. It revolves around a number of dominant theories which can be described thus:

JONES AND THE ELASTIC PREMIERSHIP

George Jones of the LSE has described prime-ministerial power as similar to an elastic band. It is possible for an individual to stretch the powers of the office well beyond their normal scope if he or she wishes to do so. Thus Wilson had fully developed his control over Cabinet, Heath had demonstrated full dominance of Parliament and Thatcher had used patronage and policy leadership to maintain her supremacy.

But, Jones argues, once power, like elastic, is stretched to its limits, the forces to reduce it become stronger. The Prime Minister who extends his or her power too far, in other words, will find that he or she will be reined back by the in-built constraints in the political system. The experience of Thatcher is particularly relevant here. Her personal authority was ultimately over-stretched to the extent that her Cabinet colleagues decided that she had gone too far. She paid the ultimate price and was removed from office.

The implication of the Jones theory is that the office is an extremely flexible one, but that it is futile for a leader to believe that he or she can make any permanent extensions to its authority.

HENNESSY AND THE FLEXIBLE PREMIERSHIP

When a new prime minister takes office, Peter Hennessy reminds us, a great stock of wisdom, experience and power is inherited. These have been accumulated since Walpole's day by his or her predecessors. He likens this to a house where the former owners have added or altered parts of the building and each new owner continues the process But how much he or she chooses or is able to add to this inheritance will vary with individuals. Thus it is an extremely flexible post.

In one sense this suggests that prime-ministerial power is bound to grow. If each new incumbent adds something to the role it seems logical that it is bound to expand over time. Yet there is a limiting factor. This is not just the 'elastic' effect described by Jones above, but the fact that the job has simply become too big for one person to handle. This is now the main constraint on prime-ministerial power.

The classic example of this effect can be represented by the change from Thatcher to Major. The latter could not hope to emulate the performance of his predecessor. She was a workaholic, an obsessive leader who refused to delegate responsibility to lesser politicians whom she did not trust. Major had neither the energy nor the inclination to behave in the same way. So he did not try. He *did* enjoy something of the enhanced authority of the position which was Thatcher's inheritance, but he used it in a very different way. Jones and Hennessy are thus agreed that the office is extremely malleable and can be adapted by each new holder. Where they differ however, lies in their description of the limits to this flexibility.

FOLEY AND THE BRITISH PRESIDENCY

As we have seen above, Foley has introduced the idea of spatial leadership into the debate about prime-ministerial power. His conclusion is that the office has indeed become *presidential*, but that it is a British model rather than an American one. He points out that the political and constitutional positions of the Prime Minister and an American president are too different to be considered to be converging.

Rather he says that the Prime Minister is playing a new role in the modern age. He or she stands out from the rest of government and is able to distance himself from it rather like a president, but does have to face the constraints of Cabinet government which the President does not. Conversely the Prime Minister does have unrestrained powers which a president does not, for example, patronage, the backing of a strong party system and prerogative powers which have weak legal safeguards.

SUMMARY

What can we make of all this evidence? Does Britain now have an effective presidency? Is prime-ministerial government now a reality? Has there been no real change in substance and does the office remain very much as it always was? These are the questions which need to be addressed. Of course, there is no firm conclusion yet. But to help us in our deliberations we can make some assertions as follows:

- There is no doubt that the British Prime Minister *appears* more presidential now. This manifests itself in Parliament, in the media and in foreign affairs.
- The dominant style of prime-ministerial government is becoming more common. Wilson, Thatcher and Blair have followed each other rapidly.

Between 1922 and 1964 it could be argued that there was only one such leader, Winston Churchill, and his position was artificially enhanced by the Second World War.

- Most commentators are agreed that the lack of a legal framework defining the powers of the office makes it extremely flexible.
- The argument that we now have prime-ministerial rather than Cabinet government is largely reserved to leftwing critics such as Benn.
- Whatever conclusion we reach as to the nature of prime-ministerial power it remains true that the Cabinet or Parliament retains the ability to over-rule a prime minister. He or she does not have a free hand. The British premier can never be truly like an American president.
- Tony Blair seems to have made a significant start in further enhancing the policy-making and control functions of the Prime Minister. We consider below whether this process will increase prime-ministerial power *at the expense* of his or her Cabinet colleagues or will simply enable the government collectively to exercise more control over Parliament and public opinion.

STUDY GUIDES

It is essential to learn and be able to describe fully the various arguments which have been deployed to suggest that Britain has prime-ministerial government. This should be balanced by a knowledge of the evidence to suggest that the Cabinet is in fact still in control.

It is important to know the similarities and differences between the offices of prime minister and president and the distinctions between their respective *constitutional* roles and their *political* elements. It is especially crucial to be able to show that there are differences between mere style and real substance. The spatial leadership thesis of Foley is an ideal way of making valid comparisons between a president and a prime minister, but can also be used to show how the office of prime minister has changed.

Exam Hints

It is one of the most common questions in examinations to ask whether Britain does indeed now have prime-ministerial government. Almost as popular is a requirement to compare and contrast the roles of a prime minister and a president.

In order to prepare for questions about the changing role of the Prime Minister, the material from this chapter should be illustrated by evidence from Chapter 7 which describes the characteristics of several premierships, and Chapter 8 which draws some early conclusions about Blair's first years in office.

Practice Questions

1   Does Britain now have prime-ministerial government?
2   Has the British Prime Minister now effectively become a president?

7

PORTRAITS OF RECENT PRIME MINISTERS

Introduction

IN THIS CHAPTER we summarise five recent premierships, beginning with Harold Wilson in 1964. In each case the principal events which occurred under these prime ministers are described, their philosophies and policies are examined and finally we look at the changes to the nature of the *office* which took place under them. In each case we can find new insights into the nature of prime-ministerial government and we can find illustrations to exemplify the various theories which have been expounded in previous chapters.

Key Points:
• Premiership
• Political philosophy
• Style
• Assessment.

HAROLD WILSON, LABOUR, 1964–70 AND 1974–76

PREMIERSHIP

Harold Wilson became leader of the Labour Party unexpectedly in 1963. His predecessor, Hugh Gaitskell, died suddenly and unexpectedly in that year. Wilson was seen as the logical successor though he was politically slightly to the left of Gaitskell.

The former Prime Minister, Harold Wilson, at
Downing Street, September 1966

In 1964 he won a very narrow victory over the Conservatives who were also led by a new leader, Alec Douglas-Home. Labour enjoyed a majority of only four and Wilson realised that he would not be able to govern effectively for long. He therefore called another general election in 1966. Labour won this with a more comfortable majority of 96. The Conservative Party, now led by Edward Heath, unexpectedly won the 1970 election, largely because of fears that Labour was not running the economy well and was unable to control the power of trade unions.

Harold Wilson remained party leader in opposition and led Labour into the next election in February 1974. The result caused something of a constitutional crisis for a few days and helps to illustrate the position of prime minister in the political system. No party won an overall majority in the House of Commons. The Queen therefore did not know whom to invite to form the next government. Should it be Heath, who was incumbent prime minister? Or should it be Wilson, as the Labour Party had won more seats than the Conservatives? At first Heath stalled, trying to form a coalition with the small Liberal Party. This would have given such a coalition a narrow overall majority. Having failed to reach agreement with the Liberals however, Heath resigned and told the Queen to invite Wilson to form a minority Labour government. Wilson accepted the offer.

What this illustrates clearly is that where the normal choice of prime minister is not clear, that is, when no party has an overall Commons majority, the post must go to whomever can command the support of the House of Commons *at least in the short term*. Heath could not do this because the Liberals would not back him. Wilson could for a brief period because the Liberals indicated they would support him for the immediate future.

In October of the same year Wilson called another general election. He could not pass any controversial legislation until he had a clear electoral mandate. The result of this second 1974 contest was another close-run thing. Labour did win an overall majority, but of only three. The Labour government survived and went on to form a pact (**not** a formal coalition) with the Liberals. The latter would support the government in any important vote on condition that they were consulted over economic policy. This was the so-called **Lib-Lab Pact**.

Harold Wilson had already indicated that he was likely to retire from politics at the age of 60. He carried out his intention in 1976. James Callaghan won the party election for the leadership in succession to Wilson, so he was now able to accept the Queen's invitation to lead a new government.

POLITICAL PHILOSOPHY

Harold Wilson was undoubtedly a socialist by inclination. He had served in Clement Attlee's radical government in the 1940s and was known for his own commitment to that cause. However, his socialism was combined with two other political tendencies which modified his philosophy. One was liberalism and the other pragmatism.

His socialism was based largely upon a belief that excessive inequality was an evil. He saw it as the role of the State to reduce the increasing difference in living standards between rich and poor. To this end he was happy to see steeply progressive personal and corporate taxation which helped to redistribute income away from the rich and some highly profitable companies, to those whose incomes he believed to be unacceptably low. He also supported the power of the welfare state in achieving greater equality, so he encouraged extensions in the provisions made for those who were in greatest need.

While accepting that capitalism has a vital role in wealth creation and that free markets are, to some extent, positive forces, he believed that the central State should play a key role in controlling essential industries and in planning future economic prosperity. He accepted the Keynesian economic wisdom that full employment – one of socialism's central goals – could only be guaranteed if the State played an active role in economic management and industrial development.

Above all however, Wilson's socialism meant equality of opportunity. He therefore promoted education at all levels to maximise opportunities for all and attacked discrimination of any kind, but especially against ethnic minorities and women.

The liberal elements in his philosophy implied a stress on the creation of a tolerant society and one where the rights of individuals, be they consumers, workers or members of a minority group, were protected. He understood that not all goals could be achieved by the collective actions of the State and that encouragement should also be given to individual endeavour and enterprise. Wilson attempted to strike a balance within his party and his government between those who promoted the State's role in *enforcing* greater equality – the left of the party – and those who wished to see a freer, more individualistic society.

In this last sense Wilson was a pragmatist. He understood how much socialism the general public was willing to accept and so held back the radical elements in the Labour Party who wished to see wholesale nationalisation of industry, finance and commerce, the abolition of all kinds of private institutions including schools and hospitals, and even greater redistribution of income or wealth through taxation and welfare. However much he might have sympathised with such socialist measures as nationalisation of land and all banks, or the imposition of a wealth tax on the very affluent, he knew that Labour would be unelectable if it introduced such policies.

The less successful element in Wilson's political vision concerned his role as a reformer and moderniser of British society and politics. He tried to reform the civil service and the trade unions to bring them into the modern world. He also wished to see the State play a forceful role in organising investment in new technology and research. Apart from the development of the Concorde aircraft and the establishment of an infant computer industry however, Wilson made little headway in this regard. Britain's position as a leading industrial power continued to be eroded during his premiership.

STYLE

If one word were to be used to describe Wilson's prime-ministerial style it would be 'manipulative'. When Labour won power in 1964 he was the only member of the new Cabinet who had held such senior office before. He had also spent some time as a civil servant. He therefore understood the intricacies of power-wielding better than his colleagues. He learned to operate those controls with great skill and forcefulness.

His governments were never fully secure. He faced an electorate which retained a deep-seated suspicion of the Labour Party and its socialist roots. He also had to contend with an often militant trade union movement which then controlled many of the party's key institutions. The Labour MPs were split into factions, the most dangerous of which was the Tribune Group of leftwingers. The factionalism within the party often spilled over into the very heart of government, the Cabinet itself. To retain his and his government's position therefore, Wilson had constantly to control the levers of power. The fact that he survived for so long with so many disadvantages speaks volumes for his success as a manipulator.

Much of Wilson's skill as a leader is well documented in Richard Crossman's *Diaries of a Cabinet Minister*. Crossman faithfully recorded most of the Wilson years from the inside. He reports a number of techniques used by Wilson including the following:

- The control of the agenda and the writing of the minutes of Cabinet meetings. By doing this he was able to promote his own views on policy and avoided controversies which might have undermined his own position.
- He used his powers of patronage fully to maintain his influence. This included the composition of key Cabinet committees and the granting of peerages or other honours. He tended to promote his principal opponents to the Cabinet in order to impose the disciplines of collective responsibility on them, effectively silencing their opposition. He was also willing to hire his allies and dismiss his adversaries when he felt powerful enough to do so.
- Harold Wilson always operated with an inner Cabinet of a few ministers (of which Crossman was invariably a member) who would develop policies outside full Cabinet before presenting them as a *fait accompli* to the formal meetings.
- He was responsible for the creation of an extended network of advice upon which the Prime Minister could rely for policy development. The term 'kitchen Cabinet' was coined under Wilson, referring to his practice of using a small number of personal advisers, who were neither ministers nor civil servants, to plan political strategy. They were said to meet late at night in the kitchen of 10 Downing Street. Among this group was his political secretary, Marcia Williams (later Lady Falkender), who was known as one of the most powerful figures in Whitehall. He also set up the Prime Minister's Policy Unit in 1974 to provide him with policy options, independent of government departments.
- Harold Wilson was a generally popular figure who understood how to use the media, TV in particular, to put across his own views. When his colleagues or the wider party were proving obstructive, he could as a last resort, appeal to public opinion to support him. In 1975, with the Cabinet hopelessly split on Britain's continued membership of the European Community, he called a referendum. A substantial 'Yes' vote outflanked the opposition successfully and the issue was laid to rest.

ASSESSMENT

In many ways Wilson can be considered as the first Prime Minister of the media age. Harold Macmillan, who had led a Conservative government from 1957–63, had certainly been a dominant figure, but he did not operate the variety of techniques in the exercise of power which Wilson did. Discussion of the term 'prime-ministerial government' could first have been applied seriously to Wilson's administrations rather than to any that had gone before.

He was the first leader who was forced to understand the power of TV and could use it effectively. He could also justifiably claim that most of the government's policies were also his own. No major policies were implemented against his will and he suffered only a handful of defeats in Cabinet. Above all he was presented as the spokesperson for the whole government. The 1960s in particular was a time of great social change. In many ways he symbolised those changes on a *personal* level.

Although his economic and industrial policies were largely unsuccessful, Wilson led governments which created more social equality in Britain, and developed a more tolerant society. In particular it was his own project to reform the education system and extend opportunity within it which serves as his major achievements. Asked by this author shortly before his death what he considered his greatest achievement, he answered that it was the establishment of the Open University. Hundreds of thousands of university graduates have cause to be grateful for his radical educational reform programme.

EDWARD HEATH, CONSERVATIVE, 1970–74

PREMIERSHIP

THE FORMER PRIME MINISTER, EDWARD HEATH, AT A PRESS CONFERENCE, OCTOBER 1972

Before 1965 the Conservative Party did not elect its leaders. Instead they emerged from a consultative process among the leading MPs and peers which was dominated by the outgoing leader. Heath was the first leader to be elected by MPs. He replaced Douglas-Home who had lost the 1964 general election to Wilson's Labour Party.

In 1970 Wilson called an election a year earlier than expected. He had hoped to take advantage of a slight upturn in the country's economic fortunes. The Conservatives, not least because Heath himself was not a popular figure and used TV extremely badly, did not anticipate victory. But they won with a majority of 30 in the House of Commons.

Edward Heath had adopted a new direction for Conservative Party policy which had been developed over the previous year. The State was to relinquish its controls over wages or prices and would not, as Labour had done during the 1960s, support firms and industries which were experiencing financial difficulties. In other words there was to be a return to free market forces in the economy. At the same time the power of trade unions was to be curbed through legislation so that flexibility in labour markets could be created. These proposals proved popular with the electorate, and the Conservative Party embraced them willingly.

Within a year of taking office however, Heath presided over a dramatic reversal of these policies. This change became known as the 'Heath U-Turn' and he never fully recovered from its effects. Rising wages and prices, together with a number of high-profile companies such as Rolls Royce reaching the verge of liquidation, caused the government to take the most direct of measures to correct these developments. Legal controls over wage and price rises were introduced in 1971. The Industry Act of 1972 empowered the government to subsidise companies which were in danger of bankruptcy. Most ironically for a Conservative administration, two companies were actually nationalised – Upper Clyde Ship-builders and part of the ailing Rolls Royce company.

The government's wage-control policy was challenged during the winter of 1973–4 by the mineworkers' union. A prolonged strike turned into a trial of strength between Heath himself and the miners' leadership. In February Heath called a general election. He hoped to gain a popular mandate for his stand against the miners and trade union power in general. However, he had overestimated his party's popularity and underestimated public support for the miners. The election produced no overall winner, but the Labour Party had more seats and formed a minority government. Heath never served in any government again.

POLITICAL PHILOSOPHY

Although Heath's government first adopted policies which were remarkably similar to those of the Thatcher administration a decade later, he himself was closer to the traditional Tory philosophy. He supported the radical, so-called 'Selsdon Park' policies because he recognised that a reaction against the socialist measures of Wilson's government would be popular in the country and within the Conservative Party itself. It was in other words a typical Tory reaction against radical reform.

The fact that Heath was so willing to reverse his own policies demonstrates that he was essentially a pragmatist, as all traditional Conservatives have been. He also accepted that an active role for the State could be justified if it was in the clear interests of the country. Indeed even after he lost office and undertook a long career on the Conservative backbenches, Heath moved further and further towards 'One-Nation Toryism', a position which recognises the need to maintain social justice even within a capitalist economic system.

Though lacking an ideological commitment in economic and social affairs, Heath did adopt one consistent policy stance. He was an enthusiastic supporter of a closely integrated European Community. He negotiated Britain's entry into the community during 1972 and Britain joined at the start of 1973. His internationalism also extended beyond Europe. He worked hard abroad to reduce the tensions of the Cold War. He was particularly successful in achieving friendlier relations with Mao Tse-tung's communist Chinese regime.

STYLE

While in opposition between 1965–70, Heath gave much thought to the processes of government and in particular the position of prime minister and Cabinet. He believed that the policy-making machinery of government was outdated and over-dominated by departmental ministers and civil servants. He wanted to establish more bodies which could develop strategic, long-term policies which were in the interests of the country as a whole, rather than those of individual departments.

He set up a network of party policy committees to prepare for government. More significantly however, he created a group of experts from outside government known as the Central Policy Review Staff (CPRS). The CPRS fed into the Cabinet and its committees a number of policy options, becoming as its title suggests, the central focus of general policy. Though it was later abolished by Margaret Thatcher it was an important innovation, which has reappeared in varying forms ever since.

Edward Heath was not particularly interested in prime-ministerial power on an *individual* level. He was uncomfortable with the media and so avoided using it. He preferred to manage government privately, caring more for its policy output than for its public image. Unlike Wilson before or Thatcher after him, he preferred to develop policy collectively. He used Cabinet committees, small inner Cabinets of favoured colleagues, and even full Cabinet itself to make key decisions. Though he supported the idea of Cabinet government he recognised that a group of 20 or more ministers was too large for decision-making. He therefore developed a two-tier Cabinet. There was a small number of senior ministers (known as overlords) who handled wider policy areas, with a second level who dealt with specific issues.

ASSESSMENT

Although Heath was successful as a manager in government, he lacked personal warmth and charisma. He was also disdainful of public opinion or of the feelings of Conservative backbenchers. He therefore often seemed to be out of touch and aloof. Yet despite his poor image, Heath's prime-ministerial skills should not be underestimated.

The journalist Hugo Young's assessment of Heath's style tells us much about the development of British government. He suggests:

Once in government ... the Heath cabinet behaved as a collectivity. It has a serious claim to be called the last which respected the constitutional rules defining how British government ought to work.

Source: Hugo Young, *One of Us*, Macmillan, 1989

So although Heath did extend the possibilities of independent sources of advice available to the Prime Minister, his administration can remind us of what Cabinet government was and can be. But since most commentators suggest that prime-ministerial power has grown at the expense of that of the Cabinet as a whole, the Heath years may be viewed as exceptional.

JAMES CALLAGHAN, LABOUR, 1976—79

PREMIERSHIP

When Harold Wilson retired from politics in 1976, James Callaghan won the internal leadership election which followed. Though he has claimed to have enjoyed being prime minister, his government, which held only a slender Commons majority and had to rely upon the support of the Liberals and Scottish and Welsh Nationalists was constantly beset by a variety of problems.

Although his predecessor had negotiated a deal with the main trade unions – known as the Social Contract – to keep wage increases under control, Callaghan inherited an alarmingly high rate of inflation. Britain had also run up excessive domestic and overseas debt, forcing the government to negotiate a loan from the International Monetary Fund. A militant faction of leftwingers on the backbenches held the balance of power in Parliament, so much so that Callaghan was forced to keep their senior representatives – Tony Benn and Michael Foot – in his Cabinet.

James Callaghan did succeed in bringing inflation down and survived the debt crisis. But by the autumn of 1978 prospects began to look bleak. The public sector unions wished to terminate the Social Contract and were demanding high wage increases. The government's plans to devolve power to Scotland and Wales had run into trouble. If they were to fail, the Liberals and Nationalists would withdraw parliamentary support. Finally a series of strikes by the public sector unions in the winter of 1978–9, known as the 'Winter of Discontent', broke out.

When the devolution plans did indeed fail, the government had lost its majority in the House of Commons. A vote of no confidence was passed and Callaghan called a general election in May, which his party lost. It is now part of Labour Party folklore that Callaghan made a huge blunder during those final two years and may have changed the course of history fundamentally. Had he called an election before the winter of 1978–9, which most expected him to do, Labour might have won (it was comfortably ahead in the opinion polls at that time). Thatcher may never have become prime minister. But Callaghan hesitated fatally. He believed the party might be even more popular six months later. Events during those six months however, destroyed the government's credibility.

POLITICAL PHILOSOPHY

James Callaghan was very much in the centre of Labour Party politics. He had emerged from the trade union movement and therefore saw industrial relations as a key issue to be resolved by government. His socialism was close to that of Wilson (see page 84), and like both his predecessors he was also a pragmatist. Though he supported the principle of workers' rights and the power of the trade union movement, he did not advocate fundamental changes in the relationship between employers and workers. He wished to see significant redistribution of income, but recognised that there were bound to be inequalities within a capitalist system.

Like Wilson he held a belief that the State should play a key role in the life of the country, providing welfare, educational opportunities, local services and controlling the power of business and finance. But he also supported the principle of the mixed economy rather than outright central planning, in accordance with the pure socialist model. He therefore opposed the extensions in the nationalisation programme which the leftwingers in the Labour Party were proposing.

STYLE

For much of his premiership Callaghan had more difficulty controlling Parliament than his Cabinet. He understood that it was vital for the Cabinet to present a united front to MPs if it was to survive in the hostile environment of Westminster. He therefore relied heavily upon the doctrine of collective Cabinet responsibility.

As we have seen above, he was forced to create a politically balanced Cabinet, accommodating leftwingers and moderates alike. When there were serious Cabinet divisions – and they were common in those years – he was able and willing to insist that ministers toed the line or resigned from office. He was able to secure the compliance of Benn and Anthony Crosland in particular with this device.

In general he understood well the opportunities he had to impose his own will upon the government – for example over the IMF loan – and when it was wise to consult and seek collective decisions, for example over industrial relations policy. For those seeking evidence of the existence of either prime-ministerial or Cabinet government in recent history, Callaghan's administration can satisfy both.

ASSESSMENT

James Callaghan can be seen as something of a bridge between the early 1970s, when collective Cabinet government seemed to be flourishing, and the 1980s when the Prime Minister came to dominate the system so completely.

He provides us with the best examples in recent times of how prime ministers can use their powers of patronage *positively*. He chose to use his role of hiring and firing to keep his adversaries *inside* government rather than to exclude them. Thatcher used the same power, at least from 1981, to *exclude* opponents. His survival also demonstrates the potential strength of collective responsibility. Without this his government would almost certainly have collapsed earlier than it did.

But though he used patronage to his advantage, he also *abused* another of his constitutional roles. By choosing the wrong time for a general election and ignoring the advice of his colleagues, he consigned his party to defeat at the polls.

MARGARET THATCHER, CONSERVATIVE, 1979–90

PREMIERSHIP

Edward Heath had lost two general elections in 1974. The Conservative Party is unforgiving to its leaders who lose elections and so it was almost inevitable that he should be defeated in the party leadership contest of 1975. What was not anticipated however, was that an outsider, Margaret Thatcher, should prevail. In fact Thatcher was a compromise winner. Unable to decide between a number of stronger possibilities, Conservative MPs chose a less favoured candidate to avoid internal conflict.

Margaret Thatcher was a surprise winner for a number of reasons. She was inexperienced having served only briefly in Cabinet as education minister, she was not particularly well-known or popular with the general public and she had some radical ideas, especially on economic matters. Above all however, she was a woman and there was a widely held view in the Conservative Party that the people would not elect a woman, whoever she was. In the event, of course, their fears were unfounded.

The general election of May 1979 proved to be a turning point not just in British politics, but in the life of the country generally. Labour's Prime Minister, Callaghan, had as we have seen above, mistakenly delayed the election for too long. The Conservatives won with a majority of 43.

For the three years up to 1982 Thatcher struggled to maintain control over her government. The country was experiencing serious economic problems, notably rising unemployment and inflation, and the Cabinet was split over how to cope. The Prime Minister meanwhile was desperately unpopular in the country. It seemed only a matter of time before she would lose power.

Three developments were to save her. First she succeeded in dismissing leading members of the Cabinet who opposed her policies. These were the so-called 'wets'. This was a gamble as it might have precipitated a back-bench revolt against her. But the gamble paid off. Rather than being viewed as a tyrant in the party, she was admired for her strength of will. Secondly the economy began to recover; both unemployment and inflation receded. Thirdly and perhaps most crucially, Argentinian forces invaded the Falkland Islands, a British possession in the South Atlantic. Thatcher's decisive action in sending a task force to recover the islands and their subsequent success turned her into a tabloid heroine. Even the communist leadership of the Soviet Union admired her, dubbing her the 'Iron Lady', a title in which she was to revel.

She won large majorities in two further elections, 1983 and 1987, growing increasingly popular and exercising an ever tighter control over the machinery of government. Although there was still a substantial minority of the electorate who disliked her intensely, it seemed she was invincible. But she made a fatal error in 1988. In that year she introduced the infamous Poll Tax, a highly unpopular form of local taxation. Despite all attempts to dissuade her she was determined to persist with the tax. It became a symbol of her own unchallengeable leadership. An election was due by 1992 and the economy was beginning to move into recession again. The combination of economic concerns and the widespread opposition to the Poll Tax led to fears among senior Conservatives that they would lose the forthcoming election. Thatcher however, would not heed the warnings and persisted with her policies. She was challenged for the leadership by Michael Heseltine, a long time opponent, in 1990. By the narrowest of margins she was rejected. Though the party would not elect Heseltine in her place, they accepted a compromise candidate again. This was John Major.

POLITICAL PHILOSOPHY

Margaret Thatcher was possibly the most radical prime minister of the twentieth century. She was, above all, a *conviction* politician. She had her own political agenda, developed with the support of a political mentor, Keith Joseph, and she was determined to *use* her position not merely to stay in power, but to change the nature of British society fundamentally.

Her political doctrine became so dominant and so coherent that it was given her name, Thatcherism. The principal elements of it were as follows:

- She believed that government was playing too big a role in society. She therefore wished to roll back the frontiers of the State and reduce its role wherever possible.
- In relation to the above she brought a number of large industries out of public ownership and state control into the private sector. This process of privatisation reduced state control over industry and also opened up opportunities for members of the public to own shares.
- In the economic sphere she was a convinced monetarist. This philosophy advocated that the State should withdraw from virtually all economic interference except control of the issue of money and maintaining its value. Thus reduction of inflation became the prime goal of economic policy.
- Margaret Thatcher believed that private enterprise was being hindered by three main obstacles. These were excessive trade union power which kept wages too high and restricted flexibility in production processes, high taxes on smaller firms, and too much regulation by the State. In all three cases she supported measures to free up business activity.
- The Conservatives inherited high levels of personal taxation in 1979. It was her policy to reduce taxation on incomes so as to encourage individualism and enterprise.
- By forcing local authorities to offer their council homes for subsidised purchase by tenants, she extended home ownership in Britain rapidly. She believed that all should have the opportunity to own property and/or shares in business.
- Margaret Thatcher was opposed to all vested interests which challenged the power of central government or which inhibited private and individual enterprise. She therefore engaged in an exercise of breaking the power of a number of institutions. These included trade unions, local government, the

traditional financial establishment, the civil service and some elements of the European Union.

- Though she promoted a much freer society in many ways, as described above, she was less tolerant of the more permissive aspects of modern life. She therefore supported the retention of traditional values and a strong position on law and order. The State was to become smaller but more authoritarian in nature.

STYLE

It is tempting to assert that Thatcher changed the nature of central government in Britain permanently. Some have suggested that she raised the position of the Prime Minister in relation to the rest of government to new heights of ascendancy. Certainly a number of her ministers whom she ultimately rejected have complained that her dominance was excessive. It became a common story that her opponents had been 'handbagged' by the Prime Minister. Rather than attempts at persuasion or argument, Thatcher had simply bullied her way to their compliance. Peter Hennessy also reports a comment by Malcolm Rifkind, one of her senior colleagues, which illustrates Thatcher's attitude to Cabinet. Rifkind reports her opening words at a meeting as:

Well I haven't much time today, only enough time to explode and have my way.
Quoted in *The Hidden Wiring*, Peter Hennessy, Indigo, 1996

But we must be careful before drawing generalised conclusions from Thatcher's premiership. There is no doubt that she did dominate government at all levels, but there is no evidence to suggest that she changed the nature of the office permanently. She was, in many ways, unique. She also enjoyed a number of advantages which enabled her to lead so effectively:

- The fact that she was in power for such a long continuous period. By the end of the 1980s most individuals who held senior posts in public service had been appointed by her and therefore owed a strong debt of gratitude to her.
- Her governments enjoyed consistently large majorities in the House of Commons.
- She was an extremely determined individual who refused to entertain opposition for any length of time.
- For the most part she enjoyed widespread public support. Even some of her opponents respected her for her forthright approach.
- She was highly respected abroad, coming to represent a resurgent British role in world affairs.
- Her vision of how she wished to change British society came to enjoy the support of the majority of the public. In other words she created and led a new consensus in British politics.

- Throughout her premiership parliamentary opposition was weak and divided. In comparison with her political opponents she appeared confident and dominant.

These are all *short-term* factors. If we compare her position with her successor, Major, we can see that he enjoyed none of her advantages. He could not therefore adopt the same style of governing and did not benefit from any permanent changes in the nature of the office.

We should also be aware of comparisons with Wilson, who also exercised tight control over Cabinet and government. Wilson dominated from *within* the system. To a large extent, as Michael Foley has suggested (see Chapter 6), Thatcher commanded from *outside* the system. In other words any leader with her qualities might be able to appear presidential. Without the favourable circumstances which she experienced, there is little evidence to suggest she could have been as pre-eminent as she became.

ASSESSMENT

The premiership of Thatcher indicates the potential power of the Prime Minister if two basic conditions prevail. These were firstly that she *wanted* to dominate government and secondly that the political circumstances were favourable to her for most of the time she held office. When Hennessy suggests that the office is what the holder wishes to make of it (see Chapter 6), he may have been referring to Thatcher specifically.

It should also be emphasised that some of her ascendancy was the result of her colleagues *allowing* her to behave as she did. They recognised that, at least after 1982, their political fortunes depended on her personal authority. Some have gone further, suggesting that she *appeared* strong because her ministers and the opposition were weak.

These views are open to conjecture but one conclusion is certain. The fall of Thatcher in 1990 demonstrates that a prime minister is not a president. He or she cannot continue to govern if the support of MPs and the Cabinet have been lost. American or French Presidents are virtually irremoveable between elections. This is because they owe their authority to the people who elected them. British prime ministers, Thatcher included, draw their authority from Parliament and the party which they lead. This authority may be withdrawn at any time.

She also made no significant permanent innovations in the way in which prime ministers operate. She did beef up the Prime Minister's Press Office and appointed more personal advisers than had been used before, but there was little institutional change during her time at number 10. Wilson in the 1960s and 70s, and Blair more recently, have made more enduring changes in the nature of the office and its relationship to the rest of government.

Dennis Kavanagh has summed up the contribution Thatcher made to the office of prime minister thus:

It is doubtful that she [Thatcher] has transformed the role of the prime minister in British politics. The office is not highly institutionalised and she has not made changes in this respect. Her significance as prime minister is that she has set an example, by pushing to the outer limits of her authority.

Source: Dennis Kavanagh, *Thatcherism and British Politics*, OUP, 1990

JOHN MAJOR, CONSERVATIVE, 1990–97

PREMIERSHIP

John Major inherited a party which was already showing signs of disunity and factionalism. There was a lingering split over whether Margaret Thatcher should have been rejected at all, and looming on the horizon were economic difficulties and the issue of Britain's future relationship with the European Union. Some leading party members wished to carry on with Thatcherite policies, while others suggested that the time for radical change was over and a quiet period of consolidation was required. At first it was anticipated that Major, lacking Thatcher's evangelical radicalism and preferring a genuinely Conservative approach to policy, might be able to reconcile the two views. These hopes however, were to prove unfounded.

His premiership can be divided into two parts – 1990–2 and 1992–7.

1990–92

In the first two years Major enjoyed a certain degree of stability. The Conservative Party and the country in general were relieved to be led by a less domineering character and one who evidently wished to secure wider general agreement on policy than Thatcher had done. Major enjoyed favourable ratings in public opinion polls and was universally respected for integrity and humanity. He also began his premiership in favourable international circumstances. Britain had taken a large role in the defeat of Iraq's Saddam Hussein in the Gulf War, the Cold War was ending and a new sense of peace seemed to be descending on the world. But storm clouds were gathering on the horizon.

An economic recession had descended on Britain and most of the developed world. The issue of Britain's relationship with the European Union, the possibility of a single European currency in particular, were due to be discussed in 1991–2 at Maastricht. Major knew that his party was hopelessly split on these issues. But with a comfortable majority in the House of Commons and two years before the next general election was due, he had time to settle into office. He needed this time because he was a relatively inexperienced Cabinet minister whose rise to power had been astonishingly rapid. Ironically the expectation that the Conservatives would lose an election in 1992 also took much of the pressure away from him.

Nevertheless Major fought the 1992 election as hard as he could. His party was unpopular, but he was respected and trusted in the country. Almost single-handedly and from apparently certain defeat, he manufactured a narrow victory for the Conservatives. In the final analysis the electorate preferred his respected leadership to the unknown and mistrusted Labour Party. But electoral success brought him into perhaps the most difficult term of office any prime minister has had to endure since the Second World War. The catalogue of problems which beset Major in the next five years were so alarming that it now seems extraordinary that he was able to survive.

1992–97

The principal problems which he encountered in this period were:

- He took office with a parliamentary majority of 21 – small, but enough to govern. As the years passed the majority was whittled away by defeats in by-elections, and defections by a number of disaffected Conservative MPs to other parties. By 1997 he had no majority at all and was relying for survival upon the support of a handful of Ulster Unionist MPs intent on holding back progress towards a political settlement in Northern Ireland.
- He signed the Maastricht Treaty in 1992, transferring a considerable degree of sovereignty to the European Union. Faced with widespread opposition to this in the party, he had to threaten resignation and a general election (and certain defeat for the Conservatives) to head off the opposition.
- The economic recession stubbornly refused to abate and, though it was a world problem, the Conservative Government was blamed for its severity by the electorate.
- The party was hit by a wave of sexual and financial scandals which led to disgrace and resignation of a number of MPs and ministers such as Jonathan Aitken, Tim Yeo and David Mellor. The so-called 'sleaze' factor was a disaster for a government which was preaching a return to traditional family values.
- A number of policies proved to be unsuccessful and/or unpopular. Attempts at a Northern Ireland settlement failed, privatisation of the railways was disliked and proving difficult to implement, and the family values or 'back to basics' campaign was a disaster.
- Major suffered increasing problems from a split party and divided Cabinet. There was almost open political warfare between Cabinet ministers of the left and the right. Michael Heseltine and Kenneth Clark – both moderates – fought a public battle against rightwingers such as Michael Portillo, Peter Lilley and John Redwood which virtually destroyed collective responsibility.

The list of problems could go further, but even so Major survived. In the middle of this turmoil Major pulled off a master stroke which demonstrated that he was a brave leader even if he was proving ineffective in government. In 1995 he resigned as leader of the Conservative Party. There was to be a contest for that leadership in which he would stand against any opponent. He promised to resign as prime minister if he lost. He told his opponents that they should 'put up or shut up'. The gamble paid off. Redwood stood against him on behalf of the radical, rightwing anti-European faction of the party but was soundly beaten. Major's premiership was saved for two years. Yet the damage to the Conservative Party was terminal and they suffered a crushing defeat in the 1997 general election. Evidently relieved at relinquishing the burden of office, Major retired to the backbenches.

POLITICAL PHILOSOPHY

John Major was a Thatcherite by inclination and indeed was seen as Thatcher's own protégé. But he was also a traditional Tory in many ways. Unlike Thatcher he believed that radical change should be tempered by pragmatism. Even if a policy seemed desirable, it should not be undertaken if the people would not support it. Thus for example, he supported the privatisation of the railways, but opposed a similar change for the Post Office.

He also recognised that Thatcherite policies had increased inequality in Britain and created a conflict between those who had benefited from the reforms of the 1980s and those who had suffered. While he sought to enhance further the scope for property ownership, private enterprise and individual initiative, he also recognised a need to widen opportunities for all.

On a broader front he sought to emphasis traditional moral and family values to combat a perceived growth in permissiveness and criminal activity. He wished to see a more humane version of the free-market, individualistic society which Thatcher had gone some way to establishing. He also shared Thatcher's dislike of the bureaucratic state and went further than her in forcing public bodies, such as government departments and local authorities, to be more accountable to the public and to guarantee high quality service. The 'Citizen's Charter', which was designed to achieve this, was his personal creation.

He began his term of office merely suspicious of the growing power of the European Union, but as time went by became increasingly Euro-sceptic. A cynical explanation for this would be to say that he was merely going with the flow of opinion within his party, but there is much to suggest that in his dealings with Europe he genuinely lost faith in the vision of a closer European Union.

STYLE

It is difficult to draw firm conclusions about Major's style of leadership. He was so beleaguered by problems in his party and his government that we can only guess as to how he might have used his office had he enjoyed the advantages of some of his predecessors. There are nevertheless a number of instructive clues.

He came to power promising to restore collective government and to build a new consensus. Some of his colleagues spoke of him being a good listener and an excellent summariser of conflicting views. He also managed to survive within a government which appeared to be falling apart around him. All this evidence suggests a prime minister who preferred to facilitate change rather than to promote his own agenda. For the first time in many years, Cabinet was allowed to discuss broad policy without the Prime Minister telling them at the outset what the conclusion should be (Thatcher had a reputation for summing up Cabinet discussions before they had taken place!).

Despite his reputation for weakness and hesitancy, Major was willing to use prime-ministerial powers to get his way. His threat to dissolve Parliament over the Maastricht Treaty and his voluntary submission to a party leadership election to enhance his authority illustrate this. But when it came to policy-making rather than mere survival, he was far from dominant.

We can say therefore with some certainty, that genuine Cabinet government returned to Britain under Major. Issues such as Britain's relations with Europe, attitudes towards a single currency and the conduct of economic policy were the result of genuine Cabinet debate. But then again, circumstances dictated that they had to be.

ASSESSMENT

The experience of Major illustrates that where a prime minister is not excessively ideologically motivated there can indeed be a return to the kind of Cabinet politics which had been described by Walter Bagehot over a century ago. Indeed Major's administration carried much of the flavour of British government in the middle of the nineteenth century.

We also know a great deal more about the machinery of government at the centre, as he was committed to more open government, revealing, for example, the details of all Cabinet committees and the work upon which they were engaged. Because the whole system was being used largely in the manner for which it was designed, he had no fear in revealing its substance.

That he survived for so long is testimony to the extensive nature of a British prime minister's formal powers. In countries such as France, Italy or Holland, where the head of government does not enjoy such unfettered powers, he could not have lasted as long as he did. But his failure to dominate government also reminds us of the many checks and balances which exist to restrict his freedom of action.

SUMMARY

We can deduce from these brief descriptions of the political life and styles of a few recent prime ministers that there is no common model of how they wield power or indeed how *much* power they enjoy. It is clearly a function of individual personality and political circumstances. While it is true that there has been a marked drift towards greater *potential* influence which a prime minister *may* enjoy, there is no guarantee that the potential will be effectively used. It is also true that there is a variety of prime-ministerial styles which may be employed. We conclude this chapter with a table showing how these methods were distributed among our chosen group of prime ministers.

Table 6: *Prime-ministerial styles*	
STYLE	EXAMPLE(S)
Consensus builder	Callaghan, Major
Domineering	Thatcher
Manipulator	Wilson
Manager	Wilson, Heath
Preference for inner cabinet	Wilson, Heath, Thatcher
Innovator	Wilson, Heath
Collective government	Major, Callaghan
Media manager	Wilson, Thatcher

STUDY GUIDES

Revision Hints

The main use of this chapter should be to provide illustrations to illuminate the points raised in Chapter 6. Examples should be noted of how the position of the Prime Minister has changed under various premiers. Note should also be taken of instances where the short and long-term constraints upon prime-ministerial power have been evident.

Such factors as the size of the government majority, the state of the ruling party, the behaviour of the Cabinet and the popularity or otherwise of the government as a whole have clearly affected the behaviour of the five Prime Ministers described. There are also a number of changes to the policy-making functions of the Prime Minister shown, and these should be noted.

Exam Hints

Examiners insist that contemporary examples are used to illustrate any answers if high marks are to be awarded. This chapter is therefore especially important as it provides a great deal of such material.

It is also the case that exam answers require a sense of *change* in the nature of politics and political institutions. By studying the experience of recent prime ministers we can see how developments have taken place. Attention should also be paid in this respect to the final chapter, which gives early indications of changes under Blair.

Practice Questions

1 To what extent have recent prime ministers been able to enhance the powers of the office?
2 Describe and illustrate the ways in which prime ministers are able to exercise control over Parliament, the Cabinet and the ruling party.

8

CONCLUSIONS

THE BLAIR PREMIERSHIP

OF ALL POST-WAR prime ministers Tony Blair has been possibly the most comprehensive of innovators. There have been others who have sought to make rapid and dramatic changes to some *aspects* of government, but none has addressed such a wide range of issues. Thus while Harold Wilson sought to modernise a number of traditional institutions and Edward Heath reformed the policy-making machinery at the centre, and Margaret Thatcher was a radical economic and social reformer, Blair has been involved in all these areas simultaneously. His plans can be conveniently divided into five sections.

THE 'PROJECT'

This is the title given to Blair's plan to keep Labour in power for at least 10 years and therefore the Conservatives out. It is very much a reaction to 18 years in the political wilderness, the long experience of disunity and four successive election defeats. The 'Project' demands political unity in government and the party. The Labour leadership has learned the lessons of John Major's shaky position at the head of a fragmented government and the divided Labour Party in opposition.

In order to be successful in this endeavour, Blair has seen the need to maintain strong discipline, attempting to ensure that all members of government and, as much as possible, of Parliament understand policy and support it publicly. Whether or not this apparent obsession with orthodoxy is the result of a determination to see the project through, or whether it is designed to enhance the authority of Blair and his office remains open to conjecture.

THE THIRD WAY

This is the party name given to a policy position lying between the Conservative economic free-market liberalism and state socialism. The Third Way proposes a fundamentally free society based largely on private enterprise and partnerships between private enterprise and the government sector. Maximum opportunities and individual liberty are to be promoted, but should be combined with a more just society and with equality of opportunity.

Although the 'Blair Revolution', as it is often exaggeratedly known, calls for strong central government and the ruthless suppression of internal party opposition to the leadership, it is also committed to constitutional reform in Britain. Most of this policy is directed at the establishment of greater democracy. Thus it is again the 'third way' between the maintenance of strong government at the centre and a more decentralised and open constitutional framework. Devolution, stronger local government, better protection of rights, and freedom of information are all aspects of New Labour policy.

The Third Way also extends to foreign policy. Here the government is determined to maintain Britain's strong diplomatic and military influence in the world, but includes a commitment to a so-called 'ethical' foreign policy. Thus the Foreign Office claims it will not retain alliances with states which have a poor human rights record, will not offer them diplomatic support and will certainly not sell arms to them. Whether or not this can be sustained in a world where pragmatism is the norm, remains to be seen.

BRITAIN'S NEW IMAGE

This promotes the impression of a more modern, younger country, open to change. It presents an open society less based on privilege and tradition than before. Blair himself has sought to raise the status and social power of people in the media, entertainment, technology, sport and high profile consumer industries. Like Wilson before him, he likes to be seen in the company of modern icons such as Richard Branson, the Spice Girls, Alex Ferguson and Emma Thompson. This new social and economic aristocracy is replacing those in business, finance and the land-owning classes who have enjoyed high status under the Conservatives.

Tony Blair's own leadership of this social movement is crucial. His personal image of the young, open-minded and cultured professional is the one he wishes to promote abroad. The party knows that he is their greatest asset (just as Major had been for the Conservatives, though for very different reasons). He has therefore made himself virtually indispensable.

LABOUR'S NEW CONSTITUENCY

Tony Blair is seeking to create a new national constituency for Labour, to attract support from those who, he feels, have suffered most under Conservative governments and the Thatcher revolution. They include the young, the elderly, the poor, those in caring professions and those who work in, or rely on public sector services – education, health, local government. It also includes the intellectual middle classes whose support for Labour has always ebbed and flowed. While building this new coalition of support he hopes to avoid alienating traditional Labour support – manual workers and trade unionists – and those who gained under Thatcher – small entrepreneurs, property owners, middle and senior managers.

The implication for policy-making is that it creates a new pressure to avoid any change in political direction which might alienate any significant element in this new support group. Once again the need for party discipline is uppermost in the actions of the government, as is a pragmatic approach to policy-making.

A NEW PRIME-MINISTERIAL SYSTEM?

We have seen above that Blair is seeking to strengthen the organisation available to the Prime Minister in his various roles. The 1998 reforms and additions to the Cabinet Office are the most important elements of this process. It is part of a continuous trend which ran through the premierships of Wilson, Heath and Thatcher. In terms of this particular book and the questions it raises, this may prove to be the most enduring change under Blair.

As Peter Hennessy has said, each prime minister tends to add something new to the office. Blair has added a great deal even within the first 18 months of his government. The machinery at his personal disposal is more extensive than ever before. He may use it to increase the collective power of the Cabinet, but it is just as likely that it will extend prime-ministerial power.

FUTURE PROSPECTS FOR PRIME-MINISTERIAL AND CABINET GOVERNMENT

A PRIME MINISTER'S OFFICE?

When Blair commissioned a major study of the machinery of central government, the Cabinet Office in particular, by Sir Richard Wilson, it was thought that this would result in the creation of a new 'prime minister's department'.

In the event the reforms stopped short of a new department as such. Yet there can be little doubt that Blair and Wilson have created an institution in the newly expanded Cabinet Office which carries the potential to become the Prime Minister's own instrument of power.

The details of the Blair changes are described in Chapter 2, page 29. In general they can be said to have transformed the rather limited role of the Cabinet Office into a newly important coordinator of a wide range of organisations which will make policy, organise their implementation and control the way in which government goes about its business. These bodies now report to the Prime Minister either directly, or through one of his close associates such as the Cabinet Secretary or the Cabinet Office Minister.

The earlier introduction of weekly planning and daily strategy meetings in Downing Street has effectively created a new prime minister's team which may well come to rival the authority of the Cabinet itself. Following the July 1998 reforms, this group included:

- The Prime Minister (Tony Blair)
- The Minister for the Cabinet Office (Jack Cunningham)
- Prime Minister's Chief of Staff (Jonathan Powell)
- Head of the Prime Minister's Policy Unit (David Miliband)
- The Cabinet Secretary (Richard Wilson)
- A Group of Senior Cabinet Office Officials
- Further ministers or officials by invitation.

When we add this inner group to the rest of the Prime Minister's policy unit – the Cabinet secretariat, the press office and information service in Downing Street – and the variety of policy units which have been created under the Labour administration and which report to the Prime Minister, we have what begins to look like a new department of state.

It is not only Blair's own ideas about the future of government which are likely to shape the position of the Prime Minister and Cabinet in years to come. The information revolution and the continued expansion in the influence of the news media place new demands upon government. The need to ensure that the government's message is clear, coherent and consistent is growing steadily. This is bound to place more influence in the hands of those who control the information. The future battle-lines between prime ministers and their Cabinet colleagues may well rest less with policy-making in the future and more with the question of who can achieve supremacy in managing the dissemination of that information.

A NEW PLURALISM

The traditional model of policy-making in Britain has been relatively simple. It can be represented as a triangle, linking government departments, the Cabinet and the Prime Minister. Most of the important functions involved in the policy-making process existed within this triangle. The many influences which worked on the system remained firmly *outside* trying to exert influence.

THE TRADITIONAL POLICY TRIANGLE

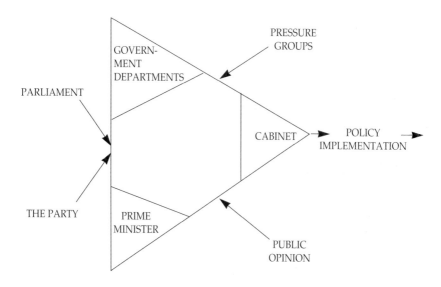

The modern reality is however, very different. The strong walls of the triangle described above have been broken. There is a new pluralism in the policy process. As well as new bodies being formed regularly, such as policy units, commissions, quangos, think-tanks, consultation groups, and back-bench committees, there is increasing involvement by individual advisers, pressure groups and lobbying organisations.

This has resulted in something of an 'Americanisation' of the political system. This implies the formation of 'policy communities' or groups of political actors who have a common interest in new initiatives. These groups transcend traditional institutions. Their members may be drawn from a variety of organisations. Furthermore policy communities are often temporary. They form to promote a set of policies and then dissolve when changes have been implemented. These groups are to be found surrounding such issues as transport, welfare provision, environmental improvement, consumer protection, education and health care.

This development is having a marked impact upon the role of both the Cabinet and the Prime Minister. Instead of initiators of change, they are increasingly becoming *managers* of the pluralistic policy process. Since it is very often the case that bottlenecks will arise in such a complex process, the Prime Minister is forced to exert greater authority to achieve decisive action.

MANAGING THE PARTY

It is a growing political truth that a party which suffers excessively from internal conflict is in danger of committing electoral suicide. Major and Wilson in particular learned this lesson the hard way. It used to be thought that, once a party was in power, its internal divisions would matter little as long as the MPs in the House of Commons could hold the line.

Today however, this no longer holds true. Major, Blair and the opposition leader William Hague have all placed great emphasis on creating party unity and, having succeeded, in maintaining it. We can therefore say that in the 1990s the task of managing the governing party and promoting the image of single-mindedness within it has become a key role for the Prime Minister. Blair has insisted that the party presents to the media a united front. Everybody is expected to be always 'on message' and rebels are quietly marginalised. This has largely been forced upon party leaders by a press which delights in attempting to detect political dissension and then criticising leaders who are unable to control it.

IMAGE

Almost as important as what the government is doing today is the image which it portrays. Governments need to be united, confident, determined and decisive, while also maintaining a caring and concerned approach to policy-making. This is a difficult balance to achieve, especially when it is in the hands of 20 or so powerful and ambitious ministers who may privately disagree on some fundamental issues.

We have seen how collective Cabinet responsibility helps to maintain government unity. The Prime Minister also has the power to remove a colleague who may be threatening to damage the positive image of the administration (eg, Peter Mandelson's removal from office in December 1998). But these powers may not be enough.

Not surprisingly modern prime ministers have developed extensive organisations whose job is to massage the image of the government. They have variously been called spin doctors, fixers and enforcers, but they all share the role of creating and enhancing such an image. Blair has undoubtedly taken this process a decisive stage further.

THE PRIME MINISTER'S CONSORT

Americans have long grown used to the idea that the wife of their president, the so-called 'First Lady', should play a major role in society. Mimi Eisenhower in the 1950s, Jacqui Kennedy in the 1960s, Nancy Reagan in the 1980s and Hilary Clinton in the 1990s have all accepted the position of women's role model to complement the policies of their husbands. The British however, have largely ignored the Prime Minister's consort. This position is, however, changing.

Denis Thatcher became the first partner of a prime minister whose role had a political impact. A successful businessman in his own right, he was able to reassure those members of the public who feared that Thatcher might be betraying her sex by behaving too much like a man. Both the Thatchers sought to make it clear that, in the home, theirs was a conventional husband-wife relationship. Indeed she made a point of cooking regularly for her husband just to demonstrate how 'normal' they were. What was happening was that the *image* of the Prime Minister was becoming increasingly important. Thatcher's image was in some ways a poor one. Denis's constant presence as an avuncular, traditional Tory figure helped to soften the image, at least for her Conservative supporters.

Norma Major attracted great media interest, ironically enough, for her very ordinariness. While Denis Thatcher had acted as a counter-weight to his wife's hard image, Norma complemented her husband's plain, honest and respectable middle-classness. She resisted the temptation to make herself glamorous, maintaining instead a reassuring passivity representing solid British virtues and the importance of family life. These were precisely the values which Major was seeking to promote.

By contrast to Norma Major, Cherie Blair represents a very different kind of modern woman. She is a successful lawyer and prominent campaigner on women's issues. Like her husband Tony, she represents a confident, cultured, talented, young professional image. In short she embodies the very ideal of modern Labour Party membership which is so different to the male-dominated, cloth-cap image of the old party. At the same time she professes firm religious beliefs and maintains a close and clearly contented family life.

As we have suggested above, the image of the Prime Minister is now a key feature of the office. There is no doubt that a more intrusive press demands to highlight the role of the Prime Minister's consort. We can therefore no longer dismiss them as irrelevant factors.

FUTURE PROSPECTS

There will be no returning to the traditional roles of the Prime Minister and the Cabinet which existed before the 1980s. That now seems certain. What is more difficult to predict is the extent to which current trends will be maintained and extended. All we can do is to summarise current developments and speculate that they will guide our thoughts in the immediate future. This final chapter identifies four modern processes. They are as follows:

- The Prime Minister and his Cabinet play an increasing role in managing a more complex, pluralist political process. They are more facilitators than initiators. As individuals they must comprehend and control a complicated web of relationships in achieving desirable political outcomes.

- The dissemination and manipulation of information is of growing importance to government. The media are increasingly influential, intrusive and informed. It is likely that a growing proportion of the time of the Prime Minister, his ministers and their advisers will be spent in dealing with the presentation of policy.
- For similar reasons to those described in the previous point, the image of the Prime Minister and his ministerial colleagues is of paramount importance. It may indeed become the case that this broad image will become more decisive than the actual content of policies themselves.
- Prime ministers have always had a number of roles to play, as described in Chapter 4. One of these roles however, has assumed ever greater importance. This concerns leadership of their own party.

We should be aware of drawing conclusions from the early experiences of a political administration which enjoys almost unprecedented popularity and has recently won a huge parliamentary majority, but the four developments described above are certainly the most striking features of modern government.

STUDY GUIDES

As in Chapter 6, the lessons we can learn from the early years of the Blair government should be applied to the theories and analysis expounded in earlier chapters. It is therefore important to note the key developments which can be used in such a way. Special attention should be paid to the enhancement of the role of the Cabinet Office in 1998–9, and to the way in which the Labour government seeks to maintain control over information flowing from the Cabinet and from 10 Downing Street.

You should also be alert to any future developments which might change the nature of both Cabinet and prime-ministerial government. The Blair government shows every sign of being extremely innovative in its attitude to the operation of government in Britain. It is highly likely that more changes are yet to come.

Exam Hints

It is likely that examiners will begin to ask specific questions about the way in which Tony Blair and his colleagues are setting about transforming the central core of British government. They will also be expecting candidates to be able to make an early assessment of what kind of prime minister Blair is, and is likely to become.

It is especially important to note the changes taking place, and any available evidence which can throw light on how the institutions of the Cabinet and the Prime Minister are developing. You must be prepared to compare the Labour government which took power in 1997 with previous administrations.

Practice Question

To what extent do you believe the changes made to the machinery of central government since 1997 are likely to transform the operation of Cabinet government and the role and poers of the Prime Minister?

FURTHER READING

ARTICLES

Probably the most useful articles for further research at both GCE Advanced level and in undergraduate work are to be found in two excellent journals. These are *Politics Review* and *Talking Politics*. Recent articles on these topics have been as follows:

Politics Review
'Political Memories of the Thatcher Era', John Young, November 1995
'The Changing Cabinet System', Simon James, November 1996
'Prime Minister and Cabinet', Keith Alderman, September 1998

Talking Politics
'Major's 1995 Cabinet Reshuffle', Alistair Jones, Winter 1995–6
'Thatcherism After Thatcher', Jane Thomas, Winter 1994–5
'Reforming Number 10', G.W. Jones, Autumn 1998

INTERNET

Government today is much more forthcoming than in the past in providing information on changes which have been made and on further innovations which are being proposed. These are readily available on the Internet. This is a particularly vital area in keeping up to date with fresh developments. The following web sites are particularly informative:

No. 10 Downing Street. http:/www.number-10.gov.uk/index.html
CCTA Government Information Service. http:/www.open.gov.uk
Central Office of Information. http:/www.coi.gov.uk/coi/depts/deptlist.html

BOOKS

The Cabinet, Patrick Gordon Walker (Fontana 1972)
Although written some time ago, Gordon Walker's standard work on the subject gives the student an excellent introduction to a conventional view on how the Cabinet operates.

Cabinet, Peter Hennessy (Blackwell 1986)
Another excellent standard work, more up-to-date than Gordon Walker.

The British Prime Minister, Anthony King (ed) (Macmillan 1985)
This is a series on various aspects of the office. It provides a useful study of some of the various arguments about prime ministerial government.

British Government: The Central Executive Territory, Peter Madgwick (Philip Allan 1991)
An exceptionally clear explanation of various aspects of the Cabinet, the office of Prime Minister and the relationship between the two.

The Hidden Wiring, Peter Hennessy (Indigo 1996)
Chapters 3 and 4 provide an entertaining account of the current state of the Cabinet and the office of Prime Minister.

The Rise of the British Presidency, Michael Foley (MUP 1993)
Possibly the best modern book on the British prime minister in the 1990s. The sections on spatial leadership are especially useful.

The British Cabinet System, Burch and Holliday (Prentice Hall 1996)
A detailed account of how cabinet works, its related institutions and the issues concerning their operation.

INDEX

ACCESS TO POLITICS

Access to Politics is a series of concise and readable topic books for politics students. Each book provides advice on note taking, tackling exam questions, developing skills of analysis, evaluation and presentation, and reading around the subject.

TITLES PUBLISHED IN 1998:

UK Government and Politics in Context	0340 71134 5
Protecting Rights in Britain	0340 71136 1
Local and Regional Government in Britain	0340 71184 1
Voting Behaviour and Electoral Systems	0340 71135 3
British Politics and Europe	0340 72079 4

TITLES PUBLISHED IN 1999:

The Prime Minister and Cabinet Government	0340 74759 5
Pressure Groups	0340 74758 7
The Environment and British Politics	0340 74791 9
The Government and the Economy	0340 74278 X
Law, Order and the Judiciary	0340 75772 8

See page iv for information on how to order copies.

GLOSSARY

Act of Settlement Signed in 1701, the Act shifted the balance of political power away from the monarchy towards Parliament.

Cabinet Committee A sub committee of the full cabinet which discusses policy in detail.

Cabinet Coordinator A position introduced by Tony Blair. This is a senior minister whose role is to ensure that the Cabinet is united on key policies.

Cabinet Office An administrative organisation attached to the cabinet. It provides logistical services, disseminates information and organises the cabinet's business.

Cabinet Secretary Britain's most senior civil servant, who advises the Prime Minister and the Cabinet on procedures, helps to draw up minutes of meetings and may help to solve political disputes within cabinet.

Central Policy Review Staff A body set up by Edward Heath in 1971. It was composed of outside advisers who considered various aspects of policy and advised the Cabinet of their recommendations. It was abolished by Margaret Thatcher.

Citizen's Charter Introduced by John Major. This was a series of agreements whereby the suppliers of public services agreed to maintain certain minimum standards.

Civil Servant A permanent official who works in a government department. Senior civil servants advise ministers and may make decisions on their behalf.

Coalition Government A cabinet in which ministers are drawn from more than one political party.

Collegiality Another term for collective decision-making. It refers to the idea that ministers reach decisions in a genuine collective way, rather than as mere individuals.

1922 Committee The name given to all back-bench Conservative MPs when they meet to discuss party issues.

Dissolution This refers to the ending of a parliament and the ordering of a new general election. The power used to be in the hands of the Monarch, but the date of a general election is now decided by the Prime Minister.

Efficiency Unit Set up in 1979, a group of advisers and civil servants who examined government operations with a view to making them more efficient.

First Lord of the Treasury The official title of the prime minister.

Freedom of Information Act A measure which ensures greater public access to government documents and reports. It is a key development in the movement towards more open government.

Garden Suburb The journalistic name given to a group of advisers surrounding Prime Minister Lloyd George. It can still be used to describe such advisers at 10 Downing Street.

Great Reform Act In 1832 Parliament passed this statute, which extended voting rights and generally introduced a fair system of representation in the House of Commons.

Kitchen cabinet A name for a group of personal advisers to the Prime Minister who meet informally in Downing Street to plan ways in which to enhance the PM's personal power.

Leaks   Confidential information becoming known to the media. Leaks are either deliberate or accidental.

Lib-Lab Pact   An arrangement reached in 1977 whereby the Liberal Party agreed to support the Labour government on most issues, in return for being consulted on key policies.

Maastricht Treaty   Signed in 1992, the treaty created a more closely integrated European Union.

Monetarism   The name for an economic policy, adopted by Margaret Thatcher, by which the government concentrates on control of the money supply, interest rates and foreign exchange rates in order to manage the economy.

National Executive Committee   Technically the ruling body of the Labour Party. Elected by the membership of the party, it enjoys a declining influence on Labour policy.

Patronage   The power to appoint people to desirable positions in public office. The Prime Minister has a great deal of such patronage.

PMQT   Prime Minister's Question Time. The parliamentary practice of inviting the prime minister to answer questions from MPs for half an hour each week.

Prime Minister's Department   The name given for an idea to create a government department whose specific role would be to assist and advise the Prime Minister. So far no such department has been created.

Political Cabinets   Unofficial meetings of the Cabinet which deal with the political fortunes of the governing party rather than strictly governmental matters.

Primus Inter Pares   A Latin phrase meaning first among equals. It refers to the position of the Prime Minister in the Cabinet. The PM is the most senior member, but does not have any *formal* political powers which are greater than those enjoyed by his colleagues.

Queen's Speech   The occasion each autumn, at the beginning of the parliamentary session, when the Queen formally outlines the following year's programme of legislation proposed by the government.

Selsdon Park   A meeting of leading Conservatives in 1969 which planned a new neo-liberal, rightwing set of policies which were to be adopted when their party next won power.

Shadow Cabinet   The main opposition party has a team of senior MPs and peers who act as the party's senior spokespersons on various issues, and form a kind of government-in-waiting.

Social Contract   An arrangement reached in 1975–8 between the Labour government and leading trade unions. The unions accepted the need to moderate demands for wage increases, in return for the government doing its best to control inflation.

Spin Doctors   Advisers to the Prime Minister, the Cabinet and the government in general who attempt to manipulate information to put the government in a favourable light.

Tribune Group   A prominent group of left-wing Labour MPs which flourished in the 1960s and 70s.

Whips   MPs or peers who are appointed by the party leaders to maintain discipline among parliamentary party members. In particular, they try to ensure that MPs and peers support the policy line of the leadership.

Winter of Discontent   The winter of 1978–9, when there was a series of strikes by public service unions causing great disruption and distress. It was widely thought to be the main reason for Labour's 1979 general election defeat.

FURTHER READING

ARTICLES

Probably the most useful articles for further research at both GCE Advanced level and in undergraduate work are to be found in two excellent journals. These are *Politics Review* and *Talking Politics*. Recent articles on these topics have been as follows:

Politics Review
'Political Memories of the Thatcher Era', John Young, November 1995
'The Changing Cabinet System', Simon James, November 1996
'Prime Minister and Cabinet', Keith Alderman, September 1998

Talking Politics
'Major's 1995 Cabinet Reshuffle', Alistair Jones, Winter 1995–6
'Thatcherism After Thatcher', Jane Thomas, Winter 1994–5
'Reforming Number 10', G.W. Jones, Autumn 1998

INTERNET

Government today is much more forthcoming than in the past in providing information on changes which have been made and on further innovations which are being proposed. These are readily available on the Internet. This is a particularly vital area in keeping up to date with fresh developments. The following web sites are particularly informative:

No. 10 Downing Street. http:/www.number-10.gov.uk/index.html
CCTA Government Information Service. http:/www.open.gov.uk
Central Office of Information. http:/www.coi.gov.uk/coi/depts/deptlist.html

BOOKS

The Cabinet, Patrick Gordon Walker (Fontana 1972)
Although written some time ago, Gordon Walker's standard work on the subject gives the student an excellent introduction to a conventional view on how the Cabinet operates.

Cabinet, Peter Hennessy (Blackwell 1986)
Another excellent standard work, more up-to-date than Gordon Walker.

The British Prime Minister, Anthony King (ed) (Macmillan 1985)
This is a series on various aspects of the office. It provides a useful study of some of the various arguments about prime ministerial government.

British Government: The Central Executive Territory, Peter Madgwick (Philip Allan 1991)
An exceptionally clear explanation of various aspects of the Cabinet, the office of Prime Minister and the relationship between the two.

The Hidden Wiring, Peter Hennessy (Indigo 1996)
Chapters 3 and 4 provide an entertaining account of the current state of the Cabinet and the office of Prime Minister.

The Rise of the British Presidency, Michael Foley (MUP 1993)
Possibly the best modern book on the British prime minister in the 1990s. The sections on spatial leadership are especially useful.

The British Cabinet System, Burch and Holliday (Prentice Hall 1996)
A detailed account of how cabinet works, its related institutions and the issues concerning their operation.

INDEX

ACCESS TO POLITICS

Access to Politics is a series of concise and readable topic books for politics students. Each book provides advice on note taking, tackling exam questions, developing skills of analysis, evaluation and presentation, and reading around the subject.

TITLES PUBLISHED IN 1998:

UK Government and Politics in Context	0340 71134 5
Protecting Rights in Britain	0340 71136 1
Local and Regional Government in Britain	0340 71184 1
Voting Behaviour and Electoral Systems	0340 71135 3
British Politics and Europe	0340 72079 4

TITLES PUBLISHED IN 1999:

The Prime Minister and Cabinet Government	0340 74759 5
Pressure Groups	0340 74758 7
The Environment and British Politics	0340 74791 9
The Government and the Economy	0340 74278 X
Law, Order and the Judiciary	0340 75772 8

See page iv for information on how to order copies.